THE FATHER'S GUIDE
TO SURVIVING WITH KIDS

by Clarence "Big Daddy" Culpepper

with Michael Kryton

illustrated by Yardley Jones & Spyder Yardley-Jones

BACHELOR BEFORE

DAD AFTER

"Clarence 'Big Daddy' Culpepper has done it again! 'The Father's Guide to Surviving with Kids' is charming and comical, entertaining and informative. From mouth-watering recipes and innovative BBQ tips to creative party projects guaranteed to entertain the Kids – a 'must-have' handbook for Dads of all ages." Gord Steinke, Television News Anchor

"Very funny!" Claire Martin, Network Television Chief Meteorologist

"A humorous resource book for Dads who perhaps lack a little imagination. Obviously 'Big Daddy' is a 'Good Daddy'!" Neal Gratton, Business Owner

"Brilliant, funny, solid recipes!" Cheryll Gillespie, Radio/TV Show Host & Columnist

"It is a fun reference to have in the kitchen and a great wee read." Andy Donnelly, Radio Broadcaster

"I would have liked this given to me at Lamaze classes for my first one. It would have helped a lot." Boyd Sellar, Corporate Safety Manager

"I read this book and realized with a gasp how little I know about domestic life. And I don't even have kids! If I ever fell in love again with a woman who – yikes! – had a Kid or two, you can bet I'd be turning to this book once a day. At least! I'll probably be using it anyway… just to get by on my own." Mark Kozub, author of "The Brown Family" and "A Calgary Album"

"The guide captures everything a Dad needs to know. It's fun and funny. The 'Jones boys' are simply the best in the business and their cartoons add to the comedic value of the book. I enjoyed it all." Marty Forbes, Broadcast Executive

"Truly a complete 'Survival Guide with smile'! Neil Sutcliffe, Newspaper Publisher

"Kudos to you. This Laundry Guidelines & Symbols page is GREAT." Grant Rowledge, Radio Producer

II

THE FATHER'S GUIDE
TO SURVIVING WITH KIDS

by Clarence "Big Daddy" Culpepper
with Michael Kryton
illustrated by Yardley Jones & Spyder Yardley-Jones

The Father's Guide to Surviving with Kids!
by
Clarence "Big Daddy" Culpepper
with Michael Kryton

First Printing – September 2007

Copyright © 2007 by Baytree Holdings Ltd.
Published by Baytree Holdings Ltd.
P.O. Box 1233, Nisku, Alberta, Canada T9E 8A8
www.Fathersguide.ca
www.Bachelorsguide.ca

Cover design and cartoons by Yardley Jones & Spyder Yardley-Jones

Library and Archives Canada Cataloguing in Publication

Culpepper, Clarence "Big Daddy", 1952-

The father's guide to surviving with kids! / by Clarence "Big Daddy" Culpepper ; with Michael Kryton ; illustrated by Yardley Jones and Spyder Yardley-Jones.

Includes bibliographical references and index.
ISBN 978-1-897010-43-3

1. Fatherhood – Handbooks, manuals, etc. 2. Father and child – Handbooks, manuals, etc.
3. Child rearing – Handbooks, manuals, etc. 4. Cookery.
I. Kryton, Michael II. Jones, Yardley, 1930- III. Yardley-Jones, Spyder
IV. Title.

HQ756.C85 2007   649'.10851   C2007-905595-8

Printed and Produced in Canada by:
Centax Books, a division of PrintWest Communications Ltd.
Publishing Coordinator: Iona Glabus
1150 Eighth Avenue, Regina, Saskatchewan, Canada S4R 1C9
(306) 525-2304   FAX (306) 757-2439
E-mail: centax@printwest.com   www.centaxbooks.com

DEDICATION

This book is dedicated to all Dads and their Kids.

Clarence's crew: Krysta, Derek, and Jacqueline
Michael's brood: Brock, Cole, Caleb and Hope
Yardley's tribe: Stephen, Hilary, Paul, Allison, Audrey and Fiona

TABLE OF CONTENTS

WHAT THEY SAY ABOUT THE GUIDE

Brat Spits:
Now that I have several children from several countries and various continents thanks to Angina, I'd be lost without the Father's Guide.

Angina Jolly:
I'm looking forward to watching someone else raise a lot of tiny Brats. And it couldn't have happened without the Father's Guide. Thank you, Clarence.

Brittly Spares:
The Father's Guide is perfect for all my boyfriends, and my EX, as well as, possibly, my future ex-husbands.

Boner:
It's a beautiful day. It's a beautiful book. It emancipates all mankind. Clarence is the new icon of Fatherhood.

Al Gorge:
Mr. Culpepper really turns up the heat on excitement with the Father's Guide. I enjoyed the very convenient truths.

Opera Whinefree:
O, O, O, O, O – my!

6

Paul Tootle Sr:
There's nothing about riding choppers in this book. How come there's no choppers in this book? Every Dad and Kid wants a chopper. I did like the tube steak recipes, though.

Pamela Undersome:
I love the cartoons. Yardley and Spyder are the sweetest cartoonists on the planet. They just bust me up. Anyway, the Father's Guide is a must for every Dad.

Ben Mulphoney:
My Dad should have had the Father's Guide when he was in politics. Because maybe I wouldn't have become the self-absorbed, gooey, TV show host that I am now.

Babbles:
There were nuthin' about cat litter in there, but I liked it cuz the cover brightened up the trailer park.

Soup Dog:
Big Daddy Culpepper,
he makes the world better,
it's all in the guide,
and there's nothing to hide,
it's all about Dad
and it's all in the mix,
from the recipes and
ABC's of dealing with Kids

Dave Lesserman:
And the number one reason to read this book? Cause it's in the top 10 of my favorite books.

George Straponmypopulous:
I could talk about this book for at least an hour.

J Limo:
I read it in the morning, in the afternoon, but especially at night. I stay up late.

J Low:
I can sing, dance and act. All I need now is a man who can do everything in this book.

7

FOREWORD

We live in a world that is placing more demands on everyone's time. Not only are Mothers and Fathers working long hours, but teenagers are also becoming a vital part of the workforce. Family members are challenged to be self-sufficient; to do their own thing. It is my hope that this book will contribute to time spent together, especially for Dads and their Kids.

Traditional roles are changing. Older teenagers are taking on more responsibilities. As more and more Moms are assuming greater roles in many professional sectors and industries, Dads are finding themselves stepping up to the plate to take on a greater share of the responsibilities in the day-to-day routines.

The key is to spend time together and have fun. Sure, it's easy to say, but not always as simple as it sounds. A few minutes anytime with this book will serve to remind everyone that life offers us unlimited opportunities for enjoyment: to cook, to play, to create, to laugh and to live life.

This is a book for everyone. I encourage you to pass it around. Share the wealth. Share life – and it will come back to you a thousand-fold.

Some notes about the content. For the benefit of readers using metric systems, I converted volume related ounces into liters and milliliters, weight related ounces and pounds into grams and kilograms, Fahrenheit temperatures into Celsius, inches into centimeters, and feet into meters. For the other more common measurements relating to tablespoons, teaspoons and cups, see the CONVERSION CHART on page 173.

Generally, you need a measuring cup and measuring spoons for liquids and dry ingredients, so they are not listed in the items you'll need within the recipes. Use your common sense here. I recommend you use different measuring cups and spoons for the wet stuff and dry stuff.

Don't be afraid to experiment. Should you come up with something different, new and exciting, send me a note; by email to info@Fathersguide.ca; by mail to me at **Baytree Holdings Ltd. P.O. Box 1233, Nisku, Alberta, Canada, T9E 8A8**. I'm always thinking about the next book. In fact, if there's something you think I should write, tell me.

There are many people to thank in the creation of this vital survival guide for Dads. Many of them are Dads. Many of them are Moms, friends, family members and colleagues.

Special thanks to Barbara Dorn, Ian Percival, Mark Kozub, Karen Phillips, Lorraine Markowich, David Markowich, Marty Forbes, Gord Steinke, Claire Martin, Ashley Zarowny, Neal Gratton, Larry Haas, Neil Sutcliffe, Cheryll Gillespie, Boyd Sellar, Grant Rowledge and Andy Donnelly.

INTRODUCTION

BY CLARENCE "BIG DADDY" CULPEPPER

A friend of mine told me, "Women are not from Venus and men are not from Mars. Women are from Earth, and men are dirt, so get used to it."

Many years ago, in an attempt to avoid starvation, I wrote "The Bachelor's Guide to Ward Off Starvation." I had so much fun, I decided to celebrate and wrote "The Bachelor's Guide to Libations". The drinking was – I mean – the thinking was that if I could keep it simple for the guys, life would be so much easier. Not only that, but maybe I, too, could get the girl and live happily every after.

Boy, was I almost right. Since writing those two books, I married the wife, jumped into Fatherhood, had four really neat Kids, picked up a few gray hairs, went through two family vans – all the while reading thousands of emails from the over a quarter of a million readers who believed I had the answer to male emancipation.

The question, which began bouncing around my head like a golf ball on steroids, was, "How can Fatherhood be this complicated?" Don't get me wrong. It's not that the Kids aren't adorable (especially when they're asleep); it's just that they have brains and mouths, which means they think and talk by default. They ask questions, want to do things, have attitudes, need food for sustenance – and generally act like, you know, Kids.

I thought the wife might kinda organize them to a point where, if I needed to do anything with the Kids, I could just point the remote in any direction and change the programming as needed. Well, that didn't work.

And just try to find a book on Kids, an instruction manual – ANYTHING –written in a language, which a guy can understand, especially when the guy is a Father, a Dad, a patriarch, Daddy-o, Big Daddy, and – yikes – ol' man! I tried to read those gooey, touchy-feely publications; you know, the ones with titles like, "Get To Know Your Inner Fire Without Burning To Death". Self-help? Self-hell, maybe.

My wife (who claims to be from Venus according to one of those books), said (maybe she ordered me, I can't remember) – anyway, she announced that it was time for me to, once again, step up to the plate – in this case, the bone-white, regular dinner plate. Despite my best intentions to cling to the couch, it was clear she expected me to get my act together and repeated as much in several text messages to my cel phone, which she sent prior to her daily aquasize class at the leisure center.

9

As my Kids stared at me (they had read the same text message on their cel phones), I realized I had no choice. It was either stare back through my cheap, reading glasses until my eyes fell out or write my way out of a tricky situation and into a new world of Fatherhood – for all our sake.

So, here it is – ***The Father's Guide To Surviving with Kids***. It's about what I (and a few other bros from the 'hood', meaning "Fatherhood") learned in the kitchen, out in the backyard and on the road. It's about transforming cardboard boxes into castles, the zillion ways to make a grilled cheese san'wich, creative ways to have a party, and the hi-tech and low-tech ways to pass the time on a rainy afternoon. It's about crisis management and what to do when the only solution is a first aid kit and your ability to unwrap a bandage from those stupid, little packages they come in.

Most of all, it's about Dads and their Kids. That's why we came up with recipes that are easy for Dads and Kids to make together. Check out the "Top 10 Tips" on grocery shopping, cooking, activities, travel, parties, first aid and laundry. Whatever you do, don't show these simple and clever secrets inside the book to your Kids' Mother. A superhero never reveals the source of his super powers or the size of his leotards; however, do tell her (or any other Mother) to get the book for any of your 'hood friends.

If we can conquer women with good cooking, then we can survive life with Kids. There are more stay-at-home Fathers than ever before. There are more single Dads than ever before. The time has come to simplify, exemplify, and demystify life with Kids.

Someone once wrote, "It takes a village to raise a child." Well, the village turned me down when I asked them to raise my Kids, so it's up to me. And you know what? Sometimes, it's hard work, but there are rewards for hard work.

Good luck, Dads! Let me know how things turn out.

Clarence "Big Daddy" Culpepper.

10

CHAPTER 1

EATING TOGETHER

RECIPES FOR SURVIVAL

TIPS TO GROCERY SHOPPING

I learned the hard way. Grocery shopping with Kids can suck the life out of you. Mind you, I did learn some things. Grocery carts travel quite far on their own in a straight line if pushed hard enough. The tweenager showed me that one. I also learned how to make breadsticks while shopping: take a fresh loaf of bread and pile all the groceries on top of them. By the time you get home, gravity will have transformed the loaf into something leaner. If you shop at a store that requires coins for the carts – yah – always carry spare change, or suffer the consequences of the line-up at customer service. Just some tips to get you started. Now, here are ten more.

1. **Make a list and categorize it**. Organize your list according to produce, bakery, deli, frozen, dairy, vitamins, and personal care. Then, if you know your grocery store well enough, itemize the aisle stuff according to the aisles. If you need to, make a list of the aisles the next time you shop, so you can create a route and know exactly where to find everything. Ask your teenagers to give you a list. Often, they know more about your fridge than you do. Keep a notepad handy near the fridge and note down the items as you run out of them.

2. **Pick a cart that works**. Otherwise, you can count on sore arms and wrists by the time you get home. If your Kids like to travel inside the cart, make sure they're sitting down. You may end up lifting them in and out of the cart several times. If you like working out when you shop, this is a great thing.

3. **Pick up the frozen items last, not first**. Especially in hot weather.

4. **Don't shop when you're hungry**. Shop with the Kids after breakfast, when their tummies (and yours) are full and everyone in the family is in a brighter mood. If you do end up shopping at a time when your younger Kids might get hungry, take along the kind of snacks you know they can handle.

5. **Get the Kids involved and make it fun**. Give them their own list and a cart. Turn the shopping experience into a race. Add a reward as an incentive. You'll cut down on the shopping time. One other thing: keep items like snacks and eggs on your list. Let the Kids get the canned goods in the aisles.

6. **Don't mix Kids and sugar**. It adds up to a hyperactive shopping experience, so avoid allowing them to try multiple, free cookie samples. This doesn't mean that you can't let them sample new items. Occasionally, you might discover something different they will eat.

7. **Make it an educational experience**. Get your younger Kids to read the signs and labels. Play the guessing game at the checkout. Ask your Kids how much they think the groceries will cost or how many groceries they think are in the cart.

8. **Know where the bathroom is and how to get there quickly**. Of course, the best strategy is to make sure they go to the bathroom at home before you go shopping.

9. **Learn about the frozen and microwaveable foods, which your Kids like**. The freezer and the microwave will save you time and money. **NOTE!** *See "BEST MICROWAVE POWER LEVELS FOR FOOD" on page 75.*

10. **Occasionally, buy one new thing to try with your Kids**. Get them involved in the decision-making process, but limit the choices to one of three new things.

13

BREAKFAST OVER EASY

The origin of the word "breakfast" relates to the fact that the first meal of the day was the time when we "broke our fast". The word itself comes from the late Latin "disjejunar", meaning "to un-fast" or "break the fast of the evening". Remarkably, the word was contracted in the Romance languages to "disnare" or "disner" in Olde French, or "dinner" in English. Thus, the word "dinner" actually means "breakfast". Confusing, isn't it? – *Food in Early Modern Europe*, Ken Albala [Greenwood Press:Westport CT] 2003 (p. 232)

Even as far back as the Roman Empire and ancient Greece, people would assemble under the atrium for eggs, sausage and pancake type foods. In 15th century Europe, breakfast was a meal reserved for children, invalids and the elderly. New world colonists introduced corn muffins and grits to the breakfast table. The rest is history, leading up to a menu of packaged, ready-to-go breakfast foods ranging from pop-up tarts to cereals-in-a-pouch.

It's a perfect world when my younger Kids have breakfast and a poop first thing in the morning. I also enjoy how my tweenager and teenager are self-sufficient, but I feel better knowing they have had something healthy and worthwhile. The best thing we can do for our Kids is to make sure their brains and bodies are fed properly – especially first thing in the morning before an active day.

For those of us Dads who do not eat breakfasts regularly, we can use our Kids as motivation. If we don't eat, they will learn a bad habit. More importantly, breakfast is a time for Dads and Kids to connect. It's amazing what I learn about their schedules for the day – things they inevitably forgot to tell me the day before, a notorious habit of which my teenager is particularly guilty.

So, what we have to offer you is a suite of breakfast recipes designed to nourish the family, without demanding a lot of preparation or execution. It's "breakfast over easy". Don't forget to brush your teeth after.

15

TIPS TO BREKKIE

1. **Fuel the mind and body in the morning**. Breakfast is the most important meal of the day. High school and college students are among the most sleep-deprived people in our population. 60% are sleepy during the day and 30% fall asleep in class at least once a week.

2. **Keep things simple, especially on a school morning**. You don't have to provide a gourmet breakfast. Encourage your Kids to be self-sufficient or, at the very least, to help out.

3. **Find out if your Kid's school has any kind of breakfast program**. There are a growing number of schools in North America running breakfast programs. In fact, the American Congress enacted the school breakfast program as part of the Child Nutrition Act of 1966.

4. **Eat breakfast to reduce daytime snacking**. Breakfast is good for your weight. For those of you counting calories, a person who needs 2,000 calories per day to maintain weight should aim for a breakfast of approximately 500 calories, with fewer than 16 grams of fat.

5. **Stock up on ready-to-go breakfast foods**. When time is an issue, things, like granola bars, mini yogurts, fruits, and milk or juice mini-cartons, help speed things up.

6. **Make a breakfast calendar**. For each weekday, let your Kids decide what they're going to have. This leads to fewer debates in the morning, when you're running around looking for your own socks, let alone yours Kids' socks.

7. **Include your Kids in the making of things like muffins or biscuits**.

8. **Every once in a while, serve donuts, despite what the experts say**. If time permits, take them to a donut shop in the morning on the way to school (if you drive them to school). It breaks up the morning routine. If you're a health nut, encourage them to order a muffin.

9. **Make breakfast an interactive family event**. It's is more than just a time for food. It's a time for information and a chance to explore opinions. Show your Kids an interesting article or photo in the newspaper.

10. **Remember to ask the younger Kids if they have to go** – before everyone leaves for school – before they, you know, go somewhere less convenient.

HARD-BOILED EGGS

STUFF
large eggs (as many as will fit into the pot)

THINGS YOU'LL NEED
pot

1. Put the eggs in a pot or saucepan, filled with enough cold tap water to cover the eggs completely by 1" (2.54 cm).

2. Bring the water to a boil.

3. As soon as it boils, reduce the heat to a lower, medium boil and cook the eggs for an additional 10 minutes. This is how you get a "hard-boiled" egg. (To get a "soft-boiled" egg, boil it for 5 minutes.)

4. Take the pot off the stove. Don't burn yourself.

5. To chill the eggs quickly, IMMEDIATELY put them under ice-cold water or in a bowl of ICED water. This helps the yolks stay bright yellow. Chill them for a few minutes in the cold water until they're completely cooled. This is important, because it prevents the greenish ring from forming over time on the surface of the yolk.

NOTE! Boiled eggs, kept in the shell, can be refrigerated for up to 1 week.

WHOLE EGGS IN A HOLE

THE "WHOLE" STUFF
2 bread slices, 1 tbsp. butter, 2 eggs, salt & pepper

THINGS YOU'LL NEED
glass or round cookie cutter, cutting board, frying pan, turner

1. Using a juice glass or cookie cutter on the cutting board, cut a hole in the center of the bread slices.

2. Melt the butter in the frying pan and lay out the bread slices separate from each other.

3. As the bread fries, crack an egg and drop it into the hole. (Cook one or both eggs at a time.)

4. Add a couple dashes each of salt and pepper.

5. When the egg is firm (after about 2 minutes), turn the bread slices over (yah, the hole, too).

6. Cook the other side for another 2 minutes and serve it up, hole and everything.

CHEEZY SCRAMBLED EGGS

STUFF TO BE SCRAMBLED
7 eggs, 1/2 cup milk, 3 medium Cheddar cheese slices, 2 tbsp. butter, salt & pepper (I'll tell you how many dashes later)

THINGS YOU'LL NEED
medium-sized bowl, paper towel, whisk,
slicing knife, cutting board, frying pan, turner, serving spoon

Let's assume you're making enough scrambled eggs for 4 people.

1. Take 7 eggs out of the fridge and let them warm up a bit. Room temperature is ideal, but even if you take them out about 15 minutes before you start cooking, that will work.

2. Crack the eggs into the bowl. Have a paper towel nearby to set the shells on, and then throw the shells away immediately.

3. Add the milk and whisk, mix, and flog the egg and milk together. As long as the egg yokes have been broken up, you're fine.

4. On the cutting board, slice 4 thin cheese slices, about 3" (7.62 cm) square (like the size of processed cheese slices), and put them aside. You'll throw these in later.

5. Melt the butter in the frying pan over medium heat.

6. Just after it melts, pour the egg/milk mix into the pan.

7. Drop the cheese slices into the pan. Lightly drown them into the mix, so they're not quite on top.

8. Add about 4 to 6 dashes of pepper and salt. Get a cup of coffee.

9. After about 3 minutes, grab the turner and start stirring the ingredients. Swirl everything around a couple of times, shovel through and turn things over. The mixture will begin to come together. The cheese will melt into the eggs. Be sure to keep the heat around medium so that you don't end up burning the milk or the eggs.

10. Once you get to the fluffy stage (takes about 5 to 10 minutes), you're ready to dish out the goods.

11. Take the pan off the stove and let the eggs sit for a minute. Serve it to an enthusiastic audience. Add toast to the menu. Like the eggs, you're done.

NOTE! *Forget the salt if you use "processed" cheese slices.*

18

GREENER EGGS & HAM

GREEN STUFF
2 tbsp. butter, 2 honey-ham slices 1/4" (0.6 cm) thick cut in half,
4 large eggs, 2 tbsp. (30 mL) milk, 1 drop green food coloring,
salt & pepper

THINGS YOU'LL NEED
frying pan, serving platter, foil, mixing bowl, whisk, turner

1. Melt 1 tbsp. (15 mL) of butter in the frying pan over medium-low heat.

2. Drop in the ham slices, and heat them 'til they're slightly brown. Put them on the serving platter and cover them with foil.

3. In a mixing bowl, whisk together the eggs, milk, food coloring, salt and pepper.

4. Melt a tbsp. (15 mL) of butter in the frying pan over medium-low heat.

5. Pour in the mixed up egg stuff. Cook everything slowly 'til it looks firm, but a little moist.

6. Put the eggs with the ham on the platter and then serve it up. This will feed 4 people – or one really really hungry glutton.

NOTE! Get everyone to chant, *"We do so like our eggs and ham, eggs and ham …"*

19

NUTHIN' LIKE A BREAKFAST MUFFIN

THE STUFF
1 tsp. butter, 1 egg, salt & pepper, 1 sourdough English muffin,
1 ham slice, 1 medium Cheddar cheese slice

THINGS YOU'LL NEED
small frying pan, fork, bread knife, cutting board, turner,
microwave-safe plate, toaster

1. Melt 1 tsp. butter in the small frying pan over medium heat.

2. Crack the egg into the pan. Add a couple of dashes of salt and pepper.

3. After 2 few minutes, break the egg yolk with a fork and spread it around over the white part of the egg. Imagine you're Picasso. After a couple of minutes, flip over the egg with the turner.

4. Using the bread knife on the cutting board, slice the English muffin.

5. When the egg looks firm, take the turner and scoop the egg out of the pan. Put it on one slice of the English muffin. Don't cover it yet with the other slice. You can trim the extra egg hanging off the edges, and eat the extra stuff – or throw it on top of the rest of the egg.

6. Put the ham slice on top of the egg. Cover the ham slice with the Cheddar cheese.

7. Place the loaded muffin on the microwave-safe plate and nuke it at medium-high power for about 50 seconds, enough to start melting the cheese. (Watch the cheese. If it starts bubbling, it's getting too hot.)

8. Toast the other half of the English muffin.

9. Marry everything together. Issue a marriage certificate.

NOTE! Make the same thing with bacon (which you would have to fry first). You can also use bagels. It's also a great way to get rid of hamburger buns.

FRENCH PANCAKES

MADE FROM SCRATCH SIFTING STUFF:
3/4 cup all-purpose flour, 1/2 tsp. salt, 1 tsp. baking powder,
2 tbsp. powdered sugar

STUFF THAT MAKES THE COUNTER WET OR GOOEY:
2 eggs, 2/3 cup milk, 1/3 cup water, 1/2 tsp. vanilla extract, cooking oil,
maple syrup, toppings (maple syrup, jam, chocolate or cinnamon sprinkles)

THINGS YOU'LL NEED
2 medium-sized bowls, sifter, whisk, frying pan, large spoon, turner,
serving plate

1. In bowl #1, sift (which means 'sprinkle') the following ingredients: ¾ cup all-purpose flour, 1/2 tsp. salt, 1 tsp. baking powder, 2 tbsp. powdered sugar.

2. In bowl #2, beat 2 eggs within an inch of their lives. Use the whisk or a fork.

3. Then, whisk the following with the eggs in bowl #2: ⅔ cup milk, ⅓ cup water, ½ tsp. vanilla extract.

4. Make a 'well' (like a wishing-well) in the sifted stuff in bowl #1.

5. Pour in the liquid stuff from bowl #2.

6. Mix everything together in bowl #1 with a whisk and a vengeance.

7. Heat up the cooking oil in the frying pan over medium heat.

8. Drop spoonfuls of batter in the frying pan. Try one at a time 'til you get the hang of it. It will be about 2 to 3 minutes before the pancakes are ready to turn. I check them after 1 minute. If they look a little more than toasty (a dark, tan-like colour), then it's time to turn the pancakes over.

9. Using the turner, flip 'em onto a serving plate and add butter, maple syrup, jam – whatever you like for toppings.

NOTE! I don't know what it is about me, but the first pancake sometimes turns out weird. After that, it's easy. Don't make the mistake of using butter in place of the oil. If they seem thin and runny, you may need to add a little more flour. One more thing, it can take practice to get them the right size.

PERSONALIZED PANCAKES

Same ingredients, but this time, make a shape when you pour the mix into the pan, like the shape of the first letter of your Kid's name. An approximate shape is fine. This isn't calligraphy.

NOTE! There are instant pancake mixes in the grocery store. Just add water.

JUICY SMOOTHY

JUICY STUFF
1 cup milk, 1 cup any flavour of juice (eg. orange, strawberry, mango)
2 tbsp. sugar, 2 scoops vanilla ice cream

THINGS YOU'LL NEED
ice cream scoop, blender, cups or glasses

1. Pour all the stuff into the blender.

2. Blend it for about 2 to 3 minutes at medium speed.

3. Pour it into cups or glasses. Makes about 3 cups worth. But if the cup is a glass, then – oh forget it.

FRENCH TOAST MINI-SQUARES

SQUARE STUFF
3 eggs, 1 cup milk, 1 tsp. vanilla, 8 bread slices, 1 tbsp. butter,
sugar & cinnamon for sprinkling, maple syrup

THINGS YOU'LL NEED
mixing bowl, whisk, bread knife, cutting board, frying pan, tongs,
serving plate

1. Crack the eggs into the bowl and pour in the milk.

2. Add the vanilla and whisk the stuff in the bowl.

3. On the cutting board, cut each slice of bread into 4 squares.

4. Melt the butter in a frying pan over medium heat.

5. Using tongs (not your tongue), grab each bread square, one at a time, soak it in the bowl stuff, and then tong them over to the frying pan.

6. Cook the squares until each side is brown. Turn them over using the tongs.

7. Take them out of the pan and put them on a serving plate.

8. Sprinkle sugar and cinnamon all over them, enough, so you have to vacuum later.

9. Put a little maple syrup on top. Yummy.

NOTE! *Kids love bite-sized foods.*

STUFFED FRENCH TOAST

STUFFED STUFF
4 Texas toast slices (the fat bread), 3 eggs, 1 cup milk, 1 tsp. vanilla,
1 tbsp. butter, stuffing (1 cup grated cheese or chopped meat slices),
sugar & cinnamon for sprinkling, maple syrup

THINGS YOU'LL NEED
bread knife, cutting board, mixing bowl, whisk, frying pan,
cheese grater, tongs, serving plate

1. On the cutting board, cut a slot or a slit, or slit a slot in the bread along one edge using the bread knife. In other words, lay the slice flat on the counter, and poke the knife in from the side through the crust, kinda like filleting something.

2. Crack the eggs into the bowl and pour in the milk.

3. Add the vanilla and whisk it all up.

4. Melt the butter in a frying pan over medium heat.

5. Stuff the grated cheese or meat slice into the slit of the bread.

6. Using the tongs, grab each slice, soak it in the bowl mixture, and throw it in the frying pan over medium-high heat.

7. Cook the stuffed bread slices until each side is brown. Turn them over using the tongs.

8. Take them out of the pan, put them on a plate and sprinkle them with sugar and cinnamon.

9. Top 'em off with maple syrup.

MONSTER SWAMP CEREAL

SWAMP STUFF
cereal (preferably a wheat or rice type),
yogurt, 1 banana, berries

THINGS YOU'LL NEED
mixing bowl, mixing spoon, slicing knife, cutting board

1. Using a spoon, mix the cereal and yogurt together in the bowl.
2. On the cutting board, slice the banana across, width-wise, to create round shapes.
3. Add the fruit on top in the shape of a face. Berries make great lips and teeth.
4. When you serve it, do an impersonation of a monster.

NOTE! Add chocolate flakes to create hairdos, moustaches and beards.

WATERMELON SWAMP CEREAL

MORE SWAMP STUFF
small seedless watermelon, cereal (preferably a granola type), yogurt

THINGS YOU'LL NEED
large and small slicing knife, cutting board, spoon,
optional bowl to hold the watermelon

1. On the cutting board, slice the watermelon in half to make a bowl shape.

2. Using a smaller knife, carve out the middle of the watermelon.

3. Slice the removed portion into bite-sized pieces.

4. Fill the watermelon bowl with yogurt.

5. Using a spoon, stir the cereal into the yogurt. You can add some of the sliced up watermelon, if you like.

NOTE! You may find it easier to put the watermelon bowl in another bowl.

26

LUNCH @ HOME

Back in the 15th century, the custom was to have a smaller meal around 11:00 am and then a larger meal, or dinner, at 5:00 or 6:00 pm. By the 17th century, the timing of the first, smaller meal moved up to 12:00 or 1:00 pm. By the end of the 18th century, the changes in the timing of the meals, which included an early morning breakfast, led to the invention of a new mid-day meal called "lunch". – *Food in Early Modern Europe*, Ken Alabala [Greenwood Press:Westport CT] 2003 (p. 231-4)

So why am I telling you all this? Because your Kids will enjoy hearing it. It's amazing how factoids about the most common things amaze them. They'll talk about lunch forever as something historical. Be prepared for more questions.

In the meantime, please accept my invitation to lunch. Remember to get the Kids involved. I'm not sure I know why, but my Kids love to take control of the creation of their own lunch. Who am I to argue?

LUNCH KIT OF TIPS

1. **Be creative**. I get my Kids to make lunch sometimes. Pretty creative thinking on my part.

2. **Don't use up the school lunch supplies on the weekend**. Unless the food is subject to a due date, you'll want to control your school-lunch inventory.

3. **Use up the leftovers**. Lunch is a great opportunity to get rid of 'em.

4. **Every now and then, take the Kids out for lunch**. Make it part of an activity like bowling. Many bowling alleys serve food. If your community has farmer's markets, take the Kids there.

5. **Take the lunch thing outside**. A picnic lunch is a great change from the ordinary.

6. **Avoid serving heavy lunches**. It puts Kids to sleep and that makes them well-rested, which means that they stay up even later at night.

7. **Serve breakfast foods at lunch**. There's no law that says you can't.

8. **Don't forget to use the BBQ to make lunch outside in the yard on a sunny day**. Use paper plates to reduce the clean up. Set up the tent and eat in the tent. I do everything intense (in "tents").

9. **Encourage your Kids to be self-sufficient**. Sometimes, it's tricky getting everyone to be on the same page at lunchtime. If your older Kids have very different tastes between them, then let them take on their own lunch assignment. I don't have time to argue, and I hate seeing food go to waste because I tried to second-guess their preferences.

10. **Turn on the radio or television**. This will get them focused and quiet during lunch, especially if they have been highly active in the morning. You can also blindfold them and serve a mystery lunch. That tends to get them focused.

BASIC GRILLED CHEESE SAN'WICHZ

STUFF
small block of butter, bread slices (whole wheat is better),
Cheddar cheese slices

THINGS YOU'LL NEED
butter knife, serving plate, frying pan, turner

1. Soften up (don't melt) the hard butter in the microwave for about 45 to 60 seconds at low power. Check it and then, if you need to, nuke it for another 15 to 30 seconds.

2. Butter one side of each of the bread slices. The buttered side is considered the outside of the san'wich.

3. Pre-assemble the san'wich with a cheese slice in the middle. If the cheese slices are thin, you can choose to use 2 slices per san'wich (or buy the thicker cheese slices).

4. Heat the frying pan to medium-high. Too high, and the bread burns too quickly.

5. Put the san'wich in the pan. After about a minute, check the bottom bread slice to see how it's doing.

6. Use the turner to flip the san'wich over. Monitor the second side.

7. Once everything looks toasty outside and the cheese has melted nicely in the middle, scoop them out of the pan. Kids usually prefer to have the san'wich cut in half or even quarters. It also helps to stack everything on one plate; looks like you cooked up enough for a convention.

NOTE! When I'm making lunch for the entire tribe, I'll use the oven on a broiler setting and keep the oven door open. I place multiple san'wichz on a baking sheet and put the sheet on the middle grill in the oven. To change things up from time to time, I'll use only 1 slice of bread per san'wich and make them open-faced. To really dazzle the Kids, I'll make iron-grilled san'wichz using – yup – the iron. I forbid them from making it this way themselves.

GRILLED CHEESE SAN'WICHZ
THEME & VARIATIONS

BASIC STUFF
bread slices, butter, cheese & other stuff

THINGS YOU'LL NEED
butter knife, serving plate, frying pan, turner

Here is a list of variations on the basic grilled cheese san'wich theme.

1. **CHEEZY COMBOS**. Change up the cheese. Try Swiss, Havarti, Colby Jack, Cotja (Mexican), or Mozzarella. Create cheese layers with more than one type of cheese. Swiss and Colby Jack are quite a combo.

2. **MEAT COMBOS**. Add a meat slice: salami, ham, or chicken. Pre-cook the meat slice over medium heat in a pan for about a minute (30 seconds per side). Then add the meat slice either below or on top of the cheese. Makes for a lunchtime san'wich sub. Bacon works, too.

3. **VEGGIE COMBOS**. Add a thin tomato slice to whatever layers you've already got going. A little sliced onion doesn't hurt. Stock up on mints.

4. **SPICE COMBOS**. Sprinkle spices on the buttered side of the bread – garlic powder, for example.

5. **SAUCE COMBOS**. Try adding a splash of sauce on the inside, like Worcestershire sauce.

6. **JAM COMBOS**. Strawberry jam and Cheddar cheese are quite tasty together.

7. **FRUIT COMBOS**. Add a thin fruit slice. Apples and pears work really well.

NOTE! When you're making the combos with meat, veggies or fruit, you may want to use the oven on the broiler setting to melt the cheese, as well as cook the other stuff you've added on top of the cheese. You can either make a regular san'wich with 2 slices of bread, or make it an open-faced san'wich.

TIME TESTED DOGS

First, a little history. The invention of the sausage, sometime around 60 AD, is attributed to Emperor Nero Claudius Caesar's cook, Gaius. In the latter 14th century, the Germans in Frankfurt, Germany created the "Frankfurter". In the 17th century, Johann Georghehner, a butcher living in Coburg, Germany, created what became known as the "dachshund" or "little dog" sausage. The people of Vienna (Wien), Austria, coined the term "wiener-frankfurter" in the early 19th century, which eventually became the simple "wiener" as we know it today.

Then, in 1867, Charles Feltman, who owned a pie-wagon in Coney Island, was being hounded by customers who wanted hot san'wichz. Because his wagon was small, he couldn't handle san'wichz in the confined space. That's when he thought about serving a hot sausage on a bread roll. Donovan, the wheel-wright on East New York and Howard Street in Brooklyn, who had built Charles's pie-wagon, created a tin-lined chest to keep the rolls fresh, and rigged up a small charcoal stove inside to boil sausages.

Feltman boiled pork sausage, placed it between a roll, and let Donovan try it. The wheel-wright loved it and the "hot-dog" was born. Thanks to baseball fans in America, the hot dog eventually took its place as a permanent icon of fast food dining.

DOGS OF ALL BREEDS

STUFF
beef, chicken or pork hot dogs, bratwursts,
buns, rolls, bread, tortillas, tacos, breadstick dough (store-bought),
stuffings & trimmings (it's endless)

THINGS YOU'LL NEED
pot (medium & large), flat bottomed steamer,
baking sheet, parchment paper, microwave-safe dish,
tongs, knife, spoon, grater, sauce brush, paper towels

Here is a list of hot hot dog configurations based on either the boiling or baking method.

Generally, a medium-sized pot filled with water to a little over half way is all you need to boil 6 dogs. Your basic baking sheet works for the oven. Cover the sheet with parchment paper. This will simplify the clean-up process. Use tongs, not forks, to handle the dogs. Never, ever, ever, ever, ever, EVER pierce the dog or the juices will run out, creating a shriveled dog.

BOILER DOGS

1. **CHICAGO STYLE HOT DOG**. Boil the dogs. Add mustard, relish, onions, pickles, tomatoes, peppers (hot peppers if you like) and celery salt. A poppy-seed bun works really well here.

2. **STUFFED WHIZ DOG**. Boil the dogs. Cut a slit into the dogs. Don't cut right through. Using a spoon, spread the cheese spread over the slit. The cheese spread will melt nicely into the hot dog. Add any number of toppings into any bun. *NOTE! This works well with fatter dogs such as bratwursts.*

3. **STUFFED CHEESE DOG**. Same drill as the "Stuffed Whiz Dogs", except, this time, you can sprinkle grated cheese (of any kind) into the slit.

4. **PICKLE DOG**. Boil the dogs. Cut a large, deli-sized pickle into thin slices, length-wise. Nest the dog between 2 pickle slices in the bun. Add whatever toppings you like.
   NOTE! A heavy onion add-on is the perfect way to motivate people to stop asking you questions.

5. **STEAMBOAT DOG**. You'll need a large pot that can hold a steamer with a flat bottom. Boil the dogs. You might want to try pork dogs 'cause they add a lot of flavor to the buns. At the same time you steam the dogs, place your buns in the steam basket. (You know which buns I'm talkin' about, right?) Check the buns after 5 minutes. When they're ready, take the buns and the dogs out of the bath and add mustard, ketchup, onions and mayonnaise. If you really want to get fancy, crush some potato chips (any kind) and sprinkle them on top of the toppings.

34

BAKED & MICROWAVED DOGS

1. **TACO DOG**. Cut 6 dogs in half, lengthwise. Cook them for a couple of minutes over medium heat in the frying pan. Stir in a package of store-bought, taco seasoning mix. When things start to boil, turn the heat down to medium-low and simmer for about 10 minutes. When you're ready, fill a taco shell with half a wiener. You'll have more room to stuff in some tomato pieces, grated cheese, lettuce and salsa.

2. **BARBER POLE DOG**. Set the oven to 375°F (190°C). Wrap the dogs with breadstick dough in a spiral fashion; you know, like the old barber shop sign. Cover a baking sheet with parchment paper and put the dogs on it. Brush them with a mustard of your choice. Bake the puppies for the time specified by the directions on the breadstick package (about 15 minutes).

3. **BUNCH OF BALONEY DOG**. Cut the dogs in half, length-wise. Lay out the tortilla flat and put 2 pieces of baloney on it. Add 2 hot dog halves on top of that. Wrap those puppies nice and tight. Wrap the rolled tortilla creation in a paper towel. Put it on a microwave-safe dish and nuke the tortilla for 45 seconds at high power. Use ketchup – or anything you like – as a dipping sauce. Because microwaves are what they're, make one tortilla at a time to ensure they're fully and evenly cooked.

4. **HOAGIE DOG**. Chop an onion into small pieces, enough to make 1 cup's worth. Take a ½ cup of chopped onions and layer them onto the baking sheet (no parchment paper). Keep the other ½ cup of chopped onions for later. Cut 6 dogs in half, lengthwise, but not all the way through. Open them up so the halves are hinged together. Lay them of the baking sheet so that the cut side is face down on the onions. Spread the rest of the onions over top and add a thick steak sauce. Bake them for about 20 minutes at 350°F (180°C). Take the dogs off the sheet with tongs and put them in French rolls. Use a spoon to scoop up the sauce and add that to the roll, too. Hoagie on, buddy!

5. **CURLY DOG**. Cut the dog, widthwise, at half-inch intervals, without cutting right through them. Put the dog on a microwave-safe dish and nuke it for 45 to 60 seconds at high power or until the dog curls around. Take half a bun, put a cheese slice on it, add the curled dog on top, and nuke the package for another 15 seconds. Make sure the cheese melts, not burns. Cover the top with the other half of the bun and watch your taste buds curl – in a good way.

PIG & A DOG ON A STICK

STUFF
1 package ready-to-bake breadsticks (store-bought), 8 hot dogs,
8 ready-to-serve bacon slices, 2 tbsp. butter,
1 cup grated Parmesan cheese (store-bought)

THINGS YOU'LL NEED
baking sheet, parchment paper, 8 thin wooden skewer sticks, sauce brush

1. Heat up the oven to 375°F (190°C).

2. Cover a baking sheet with parchment paper.

3. Unroll the breadstick dough and separate the sticks.

4. Spear the dogs, length-wise, with the sticks, leaving 2 inches of each stick exposed.

5. Wrap a slice of bacon in a spiral kinda fashion around the hot dog, and then wrap the refrigerated breadstick over the bacon. Hold everything together with a toothpick.

6. Melt the 2 tbsp. of butter in the microwave at low power for about 45 to 60 seconds and then brush the butter over the breadsticks. (You may have to nuke the butter a little longer.)

7. Sprinkle the breadsticks with Parmesan cheese.

8. Bake them for about 18 to 20 minutes or until the breadsticks are golden brown.

MONTE CRISPY

CRISPY STUFF
4 bread slices, 2 Swiss or mozzarella cheese slices,
2 smoked beef or ham slices, 2 eggs, 1 cup rice crispies

THINGS YOU'LL NEED
bowl, whisk, casserole dish, non-stick frying pan

1. Build the san'wich with the meat and cheese inside the bread.

2. Crack the eggs into the bowl and whisk 'em up. Set that aside.

3. Next, cover the bottom of the casserole dish with a layer of rice crispies.

4. Using the tongs, dip the whole san'wich into the whisked egg.

5. Take the san'wich out of the bowl and press them, one side at a time, into the rice crispies.

6. Grill both sides of the san'wichz at medium heat in the frying pan until it's crispy. Make sure the egg is fully cooked and the cheese is melted.

EASY SUBS

SUB STUFF

meat slices, cheese slices, hero rolls, hot dog buns,
lettuce, tomatoes, onions, peppers, condiments, sauces, spices

THINGS YOU'LL NEED

plate, bread knife, scooping spoon

1. **ROLLY BALONEY SUB**. Take a slice of baloney. Coat it with mustard. Lay a cheese slice on it. Add nothing or everything, which can include tomatoes, lettuce and onions. Roll the loaded baloney slice first and then stick it in a hot dog bun or a smaller roll. Voila! Instant sub. If your Kids like it heated, nuke it for about 15 seconds at high power in the microwave.

2. **CANOE SUB**. Take a hero roll. Slice it in half, length-wise. With a spoon, scoop out some of the soft bread inside. Line the 'trough' you created with lunch meats, cheese slices, veggie fixings, condiments and sauces. You have a couple of options. Either go the traditional route and cover the stuffed slice with the other half of the bun, or make it an open faced CANOE-SUB, which means you can line the other half of the bun and make two, open-faced subs. You might want to sprinkle a little vegetable oil and red wine vinegar on top to juice up the veggies.

NOTE! *CANOE SUBS serve as the basis for just about any sub you want to make.*

37

SLINKY SUB

SLINKY STUFF

Italian or French loaf, 5 oz. (150 g) thin chicken or turkey slices,
3 oz. (85 g) sliced ham, 6 oz. (170 g) Cheddar cheese slices
(or Monterey Jack), 1/4 cup mayonnaise or salad dressing,
1 tbsp. Italian dressing,
1 tbsp. grated Parmesan cheese (store-bought)

THINGS YOU'LL NEED

bread knife, cutting board, baking sheet, parchment paper,
mixing bowl, mixing spoon

1. This recipe is designed for 6 san'wichz (which means 13 slices). Don't include the crust tips in the count. On the cutting board, slice the loaf, width-wise (like you were making toast), leaving one side hinged. So don't slice it all the way through.

2. Cover a baking sheet with parchment paper and put the sliced (hinged) loaf on it.

3. Fill each "stuffing" slice (slices # 2, 4, 6, 8, 10, 12) with chicken or turkey, ham, and cheese slices. (Try to see individual san'wichz in your mind to figure it out.)

4. In a bowl, mix the mayonnaise or salad dressing, Italian dressing, and grated Parmesan cheese.

5. Add a tsp. of this mix on top of the meat in every "stuffing" slice.

6. Heat up the oven up to 375°F (190°C) and bake the sub for 15 minutes.

PIZZA SUB

PIZZA STUFF

four 6-inch (15 cm) sub rolls, 1 jar pizza sauce (store-bought),
1/4 cup grated mozzarella cheese (store-bought),
deli pepperoni (enough to cut 24 slices)

THINGS YOU'LL NEED

bread knife, cutting board, microwave-safe dish, paper towel, spoon,
baking sheet, parchment paper

1. On the cutting board, slice open the sub rolls. Don't separate the halves. Keep them hinged.

2. Pour 3 cups of pizza sauce into the microwave-safe dish. Cover it with a paper towel.

3. Microwave the sauce for about 2 minutes at HIGH power. Check it, stir, and nuke for another minute if the sauce is not consistently hot.

4. Spoon the sauce into the rolls.

5. Sprinkle a ¼ cup of mozzarella cheese over the sauce.

6. Stuff each roll with 6 slices of pepperoni.

7. Cover a baking sheet with parchment paper and put the rolls on it.

8. Bake them in the oven for 15 minutes at 375°F (190°C).

CHEDDAR SOUP

The first soup dates back to 6000 B.C. (Before Campbell's?), with the main ingredient being Hippopotamus and other animal bones. The English word "soup" comes from the old word "sop", which is a slice of bread covered with beef roast juices. Why am I telling you this? Because it helps to kill the time while making soup.

SOUP STUFF
3 tbsp. all-purpose flour, 3 tbsp. softened butter, 2 cups milk,
1 cup chicken broth,
salt & pepper, 6 oz. (170 g) finely grated Cheddar cheese

THINGS YOU'LL NEED
pot, whisk, cheese grater

1. Soften the butter and then, in a pot over medium heat, whisk the flour and butter together.

2. Heat it for about 20 seconds.

3. Slowly whisk in the milk and then whisk in the chicken broth.

4. Cook it until the soup bubbles and thickens a little. Grate the cheese while you're waiting.

5. Throw in some dashes of salt and pepper.

6. Take the pot off the stove and, using the whisk, stir in the grated cheese until it has melted.

NOTE! About the "whisk" versus the "spoon". The whisk breaks up the ingredients better because of its design. But there's nothing on the planet stopping you from using a spoon.

40

GETRIDOFIT SOUP

SOUP STUFF
veggies in the fridge that need to be used up (carrots, celery & onions), chicken noodle soup, (options: tomato or beef noodle)

THINGS YOU'LL NEED
slicing knife, cutting board, pot

1. On the cutting board, slice up the veggies into smaller than average, bite-sized pieces.

2. Pour the un-heated soup into the pot.

3. Add the sliced veggies into the pot.

4. Heat up the soup. Voila! Chicken/tomato/beef vegetable soup.

NOTE! *You can add potatoes. See the DINNER section (pg. 71) to find out how you prepare potatoes.*

FISHY TOAST

FISHY STUFF
1 lb. (500 g) firm-fleshed fish fillet (cod works well),
1 pressed clove garlic, 3 tbsp. minced onion, 1 1/4 tsp. grated fresh ginger,
1 egg, 1^1/$_2$ tsp. cornstarch, 1 tsp. soy sauce, 1 tbsp. sherry,
12 white bread slices, 1 tbsp. cooking oil,

THINGS YOU'LL NEED
mincing knife, peeler, garlic press, grater, mixing bowl, mixing spoon or
fork, bread knife, cutting board, frying pan, turner, paper towel

1. Mince the fish. Don't mince your words. Mincing is your opportunity to take all the anger you've ever had in your life and direct it at the fish. In other words, beat the crap out of it.

2. On the cutting board, press the garlic (peel it first), mince the onion (peel it first), and grate the ginger (peel it first).

3. With a spoon or fork, mix all the ingredients in the bowl except the bread and the oil.

4. On the cutting board, cut off the bread crusts and then cut each slice of bread into 4 squares.

5. Spread the mixture on the bread. Use the spoon.

6. Heat the pan to medium-high and drop in the oil. Heat up the oil for a couple of minutes.

7. Fry each piece, fish-side down, until brown. Use the turner to flip it over and brown the other side.

8. Dab the excess liquid off with paper towels. Don't eat the towel.

OUT TO LUNCH

Okay, I tricked my Kids. I asked them to bring me a complete list of every item on the school cafeteria menu and coin food machines with the promise that I would give them enough money to have anything they wanted for lunch at school.

Yikes! The lists they brought back were recipes for nutritional disaster. Not every school is completely up to speed on the healthy, school-lunch program thing. Hot dogs, chips and twinkie treat cakes do not a healthy school lunch make. But, I'm sure the cafeteria food suppliers and the machine vendors feel like they died and went to heaven.

The world is worried about drugs in school and, meanwhile, we're letting our Kids pump sugar and fat into their veins. But, I know what it's like for a Dad to scramble on a school day morning. Despite the constant self-reminders the night before to prepare school lunches, you find yourself panicking minutes before the school bus hits your Kid's stop. Of course, you can throw lunch money at the Kids; but, the cost is the guilt you feel later in the day, especially at lunch, when you imagine your child ordering French Fries and gravy at the cafeteria counter.

Wait! There's hope yet! According to research by them (all the experts who we think live perfect lives), a Dad can make the school lunch experience easier and healthier.
Just follow my guidelines and point the Kids towards the fridge and pantry.

TIPS TO SCHOOL LUNCH

1. **Let the Kids make their own lunch whenever they want**. Know what? They love it!

2. **Let your Kids pick out their own school lunch kits**. It helps them take ownership of their lunch thing. They'll even want to use the kit.

3. **Simplify lunch**. Kids love san'wichz more than anything else. No forks, spoons or knives. The less complicated lunch is, the greater the chances they'll consume it.

4. **Use zip-type bags and plastic containers in all sizes**. They're the most important inventions ever to hit the market. Plus, if you freeze juices that come in cardboard containers, you can use them to keep san'wichz fresh. They'll thaw in time for lunch.

5. **Explore new lunch snacks**. Lunch is a time to experiment; the key to discovering new snacks. The beauty of the lunch kit is that the Kids don't throw anything away. They just leave it in the lunch kit to ferment. If snacks come back, then they didn't work. Even major corporations, like airlines, analyze garbage to see what people throw away. See? It's an education. In this case, if it comes back to you, they didn't like it.

6. **Leave a coin in the lunch kit**. Every now and then, let them indulge in the coin-operated, food machine experience. They can choose to save the coins for something else, too.

7. **Avoid stocking the lunch kit with anything (besides the san'wich) that will melt or wilt**. Pack the veggies in a plastic container, rather than a plastic wrap. There is no such thing as "cling-free". It all clings. Assume that anything that needs to be wrapped like an Egyptian mummy will never be unwrapped.

8. **Buy pre-packaged lunches in easy-to-open packages**. On those days when everyone is in a rush, the grab-and-pack strategy saves your bacon – and theirs. Don't pack bacon.

9. **Once in a while, take them out for lunch**. It breaks up their routine – and yours.

10. **Teach your Kids to refrain from sharing lunch**. Explain the dangers of allergies.

NOTE! Remember to wave as they head off to school.

44

SKOOL SAN'WICHZ

I assume that most Dads and Kids know how to make basic san'wichz: peanut butter and jelly, ham and cheese – and you can definitely pack some of the subs we feature in the previous section. ***NOTE!*** *See pages 37 to 39.*

So here are some slightly different san'wichz, which are easy to make, and easy for the Kids to handle and consume at school.

ROLL 'N ROCK SAN'WICHZ

SAN'WICH BREAD STUFF THAT CAN BE ROLLED
cracker bread, tortilla wraps, crustless bread

SAN'WICH STUFFINGS THAT CAN ROCK
deli meats, spreads, condiments, lettuce

THINGS YOU'LL NEED
bread knife, cutting board, spoon, toothpicks, rock 'n roll tunes

NOTE! All of these san'wichz can be rolled. As long as you fold the ends over, you can make any kind of stuffing without worrying about your Kid making a mess. You can also slice rolls into smaller sections to create bite-sized finger foods. You might need toothpicks to hold 'em together.

1. **TUNA WRAP**. Bread: cracker bread. Stuffing: tuna and mayonnaise. Add onion and mozzarella if your Kid likes that sort of stuff.

2. **CHICKEN WRAP**. Bread: tortilla wrap. Stuffing: store-bought deli chicken salad. You're done.

3. **LEAF LINER WRAP**. Bread: tortilla wrap. Stuffing: anything inside a lettuce leaf, like grated cheese or chopped meat or both.

4. **MEAT FINGER WRAP**. Bread: tortilla wrap. Stuffing: pre-cooked ground beef shaped like a finger. You can also use finger-length chicken slices. In fact, any meat shaped something like a finger will work. Avoid using your own fingers.

5. **DELI WRAP**. Bread: any basic bread without the crust. Stuffing: any deli meat with or without a cheese slice. Rolls real easy.

6. **SPREAD WRAP**. Bread: any basic bread without the crust. Spread: your choice: cream cheese, cheese spread, peanut butter, jam, or avocado. Thicker is better.

NOTE! Once you've rolled a wrap stuffed with a softer spread, you'll have to close off both ends of the wrap, otherwise the spread will – well – spread. You can seal the ends with a small, round slice of garlic coil meat or pepperoni stick.

LAST NOTE! Any of these san'wichz works for lunch @ home. In fact, you can create a bit of a smorgasbord and roll out a variety of 'wichz. Now you're ready to rock!

46

ROLL 'N ROCK <u>NON</u> - SAN'WICHZ

<u>NON-SAN'WICH STUFFINGS THAT YOU CAN STILL ROLL</u>
deli meats, cheese slices, thick spreads, lettuce

<u>THINGS YOU'LL NEED</u>
knife, plate, spoon, toothpicks, rap tunes

1. **MEAT WRAP**. Take any deli meat slice and roll a cheese slice inside.
2. **CHEESE WRAP**. Wrap a thick spread inside a slice of cheese.
4. **LEAF WRAP**. Wrap a piece of cheese or thick spread inside a lettuce leaf.

FINGER FOOD LUNCHES

Finger food lunches are about bringing together a balanced combination of things that your Kids will consume willingly. You'll also save time preparing school lunches.

FINGER FOOD STUFF

crunchy veggies (celery, broccoli, carrots), left over pizza dips, salad dressing, mini-cheese packages, crackers, muffins, cookies, fruit, yogurt, box juices, chips

THINGS YOU'LL NEED

zip-type bags, plastic containers, toothpicks, plastic spoons

1. Pre-cut the veggies so you or the Kids can grab it and put it in a small container.

2. Save your delivery pizza dips for the veggies – or use salad dressings in small containers.

3. Buy the small-pre-packed cheeses. Once again, the Kids can choose what they want.

4. Figure out what kinds of crackers your Kids like and always have them in stock.

5. Muffins or cookies can round out a lunch menu.

6. If your Kids like fruit, make sure you keep the fridge freshly stocked. Buy smaller apples and pears.

7. Juice boxes are easy to stock. You can freeze them, too. When they're packed frozen in the lunch kit, they'll keep lunches cool in the locker. This keeps yogurt or fruit fresh for lunch. By lunchtime, the juice boxes will have thawed out. It all works.

8. There's nothing wrong with chips. The kettle-fried chips contain no trans fat.

48

DINNER'S ON: AND NOW THE NEWS

At the end of a hard work day – and they're all hard – the last thing I want to do is make dinner. Unless you enjoy cooking or are the next cooking show waiting to happen, dinner is a challenge. Between the finicky taste buds of Kids and the pressure of time, making dinner can feel like a marathon. I learned the hard way. I learned by accident. Now, I have the opportunity to help you.

Like any other meal, dinner can be a very special time with your Kids, because dinnertime offers significant opportunities for Dads to shine – or whine – if you're so inclined. Hey! Life isn't always perfect. Like I've said many times to my Kids (just to confuse them), "Perfection is imperfection at work."

If we take a page from the Italian culture, dinner is an event that can last for hours. It's about connecting with everyone to get the news of the day. This is probably why television has a news hour around dinnertime. Whether you see your Kids everyday, or you see them on a schedule, the big meal of the day can become the big deal of the day without transforming you into the Iron Chef.

The key to success is to involve your Kids and use distractions, creatively. I like to turn on the news and have it on in the background. My Kids love to watch me talk to the TV, as I share my comments with no one in particular about what I think of the various news stories. Instead of me asking questions of them – like, "What did you learn today?" – my Kids question me. "Why did you say that, Daddy?" "What do you mean the world is going to hell in a hand basket?" "Why did you say that woman is self absor – ab – what's that word?"

While I explain to them the reason why politicians are idiots and that everything causes cancer, I slip in the odd request. "Could you grab the ketchup out of the fridge?" "Can you pour some juice or milk and ask everyone what they want." "Who wants to stir the rice?" "Somebody grab plates and stuff to set the table."

As they mindlessly perform these tasks, the dialogue continues with no restraint. Somewhere between the questions and answers, the table gets set, liquids are dispensed, and, together, we have cured the world of all its diseases, eradicated starvation from the planet, and figured out how to make a time machine. It has become a ritual. We've become a show at dinner. "Dad, are we going to yell at the TV today?" You bet we will.

Sometimes, I ask them questions, but not the open-ended, touchy-feely dribble that comes from the clinically sterile, detached therapists and psychologists. My questions are ridiculous. "Who wants to invent a time machine?" "Where and when would we go with it?" "If you could make the weirdest san'wich, what would you put on it?" "Let's try making it."

Kids are spontaneous. Their focus shifts with no notice. Don't fight it. Go with it.

TIPS TO DINNER

1. **Stuff the freezer with easy-to-bake food**. They're fast, too: chicken fingers, fish fingers, pizzas, hot dogs, quick-bake French Fries with 0 trans fat, and frozen vegetables, like peas and corn. I'm not suggesting that this is the definitive diet. This is the quick stuff. Baking gives you time to focus on other things or just relax before dinner and yell at the TV.

2. **Use parchment paper when cooking with the oven**. It'll save a whack-load of time on the cleaning. Instead of putting food directly on the baking sheets, put them on the parchment paper that can be used on a baking sheet in the oven. After dinner, all you have to do is throw the paper out, quickly wipe the baking sheet, and you're done, buddy.

3. **Buy lots of packaged food staples**. Different flavors of rice, noodles, hamburger helpers or side dishes can be mixed and matched according to the main feature of the meal.

4. **Save those unused dips you get with the delivery pizzas**. Put them in the freezer for future use. Fresh vegetables can be a challenge with Kids. It's all in the dip. Thick salad dressings make for a good dip. No preparation required.

5. **Learn everything you can about microwaveable foods**. The menu of items out there is amazing. There are so many nutritional dinners that are ready to go. If you have a busy evening schedule (soccer, dance, gymnastics, hockey, football, cheerleading, driving lessons, parent-teacher interviews – and that's just for your teenager on Tuesday), you will have a need for speed. ***NOTE!*** *See "BEST MICROWAVE POWER LEVELS FOR FOOD" on page 75.*

6. **Try new things with your Kids**. Let the Kids pick those new things out when you're grocery shopping. Worst-case scenario, you'll end up eating it yourself.

7. **Every now and then, have a camp-styled meal**. There's nothing like hot dogs with potato chips. Nutritionalists might cringe, but you can buy whole-wheat buns for the dogs and kettle-fried chips.

8. **Don't pressure yourself with variety**. If your Kids like something routinely on a Friday night – pizza, for instance – then, stick with it.

9. **Give yourself a break when you need it**. Fast food chains have healthier choices these days.

10. **Recruit the Kids in the clean-up**. Get them in the habit of rinsing their own dishes or putting them where you need them to do it yourself. Kids learn good habits quickly.

And now the news. Dinner's ready. Just like that.

AUNT LORRAINE CULPEPPER'S
HURRY UP CHICKEN

HURRY UP STUFF
1 cup ketchup, $1/2$ cup water, $1/2$ cup brown sugar, 1 package dry onion soup mix, 3 lbs. (1.5 kg) chicken (boneless breasts are the best)

THINGS YOU'LL NEED
mixing spoon, mixing bowl, casserole dish with lid

1. Don't pre-make the soup. Using a spoon, mix the ketchup, water, sugar and dry (unmade), onion soup mix in a bowl.
2. Put the chicken in the casserole dish.
3. Add the bowl mixture to the casserole and cover it with a lid.
4. Preheat the oven to 350°F (180°C).
5. Bake the covered chicken for $1\frac{1}{2}$ hours in the oven.

WINGS ON FIRE

FIRE STUFF
30 chicken wings, 5 tbsp. hot sauce, BBQ sauce, salt & pepper

THINGS YOU'LL NEED
large bowl, baking pan, foil, sauce brush

1. Toss the wings into the bowl.
2. Sprinkle the hot sauce over the chicken.
3. Put the wings in the fridge for an hour.
4. Take the bowl out of the fridge and drain the extra liquid or sauce out of the bowl.
5. Take the wings out of the bowl and lay them on the baking pan.
6. Cover the pan with foil.
7. Heat the oven to 375°F (190°C).
8. Bake the chicken wings for 40 minutes.
9. Take out the pan and drain the liquid off the pan.
10. Using the sauce brush, coat the wings with BBQ sauce. Add dashes of salt & pepper.
12. Bake the wings for another 15 minutes.

NOTE! *This goes great with potato salad or fries.*

WHOLY CHICKEN

CHICKEN STUFF
1 whole chicken, 1 tbsp. butter, salt & pepper,
spices that go with chicken (dill, oregano, sage, poultry seasoning)

THINGS YOU'LL NEED
roasting pan

1. Wash the chicken.

2. Rub the chicken with butter.

3. Sprinkle salt and pepper and the spices of your choice all over the chicken.

4. Heat the oven to 350°F (180°C).

5. Put the chicken into a roasting pan and cook it in the oven for an hour.

PIG CHOPS

PIG STUFF
2 tbsp. oil, four 1/2-inch (1.27 cm) thick pork loin chops,
1 green pepper, 1 cup pineapple juice (unsweetened), 1 tbsp. brown sugar,
1/2 tsp. salt, 1 tbsp. cornstarch

THINGS YOU'LL NEED
frying pan, pan cover, corning ware dish, chopping knife, cutting board,
mixing spoon, small bowl

1. On the stove, heat the oil in the pan and, when it's hot enough, sear both sides of the pork chops.

2. Move the chops into a corningware dish and keep them warm in the oven.

3. Chop up the green pepper on the cutting board.

3. Add the green pepper, sugar, salt, and a ¼ cup pineapple juice to the frying pan and stir it up.

4. Move the pork chops back into the pan from the corningware dish.

5. Cover the pan and cook the chops on the stove for 20 minutes at medium heat.

6. Use a spoon to mix the cornstarch with the other ¾ cup of pineapple juice in a small bowl.

7. Add the cornstarch mixture. Stir it around until the sauce is thick.

NOTE! Goes great with rice and a veggie.

54

BASIC BONELESS PIGGY

PIGGY STUFF
boneless ham 5 to 6 lb. (2.2 to 2.5 kg) to feed 4 people,
or you can buy a half ham instead of a whole ham,

GLAZE OPTION:
6 oz. (177 mL) thawed orange juice concentrate, 1/2 cup honey

THINGS YOU'LL NEED
shallow oven pan, meat thermometer, mixing spoon, lots of ham-it-up jokes

1. Put the ham in a shallow pan and cook it uncovered in the oven for 75 to 90 minutes at 350°F (180°C) or until an inserted meat thermometer reads 140°F (60°C). It works out to about 15 to 18 minutes per pound (per 500 g).

2. If you want a glaze, glaze your ham with a mixture of honey and orange juice concentrate during the last 15 minutes of reheating. Use a spoon to mix and distribute the glaze.

NOTE! This puppy – or piggy – will give you plenty of leftovers and options after the fact: hamwichz, ham snacks – you name it.

BASIC ROAST BEAST

BEAST STUFF
3 lb. (1.5 kg) eye-of-round beef roast,
1/2 tsp. salt, 1/2 tsp. garlic powder, 1/4 tsp. freshly ground black pepper

THINGS YOU'LL NEED
cotton twine, shallow baking pan, pepper grinder, foil

1. Heat the oven up to 375°F (190°C).

2. Most grocery stores tie the beast with string to hold it together, BUT, if the beast is untied, tie it with cotton twine at 3 inches (7.6 cm) apart.

3. Put the beast in the pan.

4. Season the beast with the salt, garlic powder, and pepper.

5. Roast the beast in the oven for 60 minutes (20 minutes per pound/454 g).

6. Take the beast out of the oven and cover it loosely with foil. You and the beast can rest for 15 to 20 minutes.

NOTE! *Like the ham, this beast will provide you with roast beast san'wichz in your immediate future.*

REALLY REALLY BASIC MEATBALLS

STUFF TO MAKE 24 MEATBALLS

1 small onion, chopped fine (about 1/4 cup), 1 lb. (500 g) ground beef,
1 egg, 1/3 cup dry bread crumbs, 1/4 cup milk,
1 tsp. what's-this-here (Worcestershire) sauce,
3/4 tsp. salt, 1/4 tsp. pepper, 1/2 tsp. allspice, 1 tbsp. cooking oil

THINGS YOU'LL NEED

chopping knife, cutting board, mixing bowl, mixing fork, spoon,
large frying pan

1. Chop the onions on the cutting board.

2. Mix all the ingredients.

3. Using a spoon and your fingers (wear plastic gloves for hygiene), shape the mixture into 1½" (4 cm) balls .

4. Heat the oil in the frying pan.

5. Cook the meatballs at a medium heat until they're brown, about 20 minutes. Drain the fat.

NOTE! *You can freeze your balls and bring them out whenever the mood hits you. The fast way to create any dish with meatballs is to combine them with sauces and soups: Italian sauce, mushroom soup – anything thick. Just pour the soup or sauce into the frying pan, heat it, and add the balls. Reheat the balls in the oven or microwave at medium-high power for about a minute before plopping them into the pan. Then serve them over some kind of pasta. Noodles usually work. You can even mix them into cheese and macaroni dinners or other pastas – spaghetti, shells, penne, linguini – anything goes with meatballs.*

DO YOU HAVE TO REMIND ME YOU'RE MY SIBLINGS!

REALLY REALLY REALLY
BASIC CASSEROLE

CASSEROLE STUFF

1 lb. (500 g) lean ground beef, 10 oz. (284 mL) can cream of mushroom
soup, 1 cup milk, 3/4 cup quick-cooking rice, salt & pepper,
6 oz. (170 g) grated Cheddar cheese

THINGS YOU'LL NEED

frying pan, strainer, paper towel, mixing bowl, whisk, mixing spoon,
non-stick spray, baking pan, cheese grater, wire rack

1. Cook the ground beef in the frying pan over medium-high heat.

2. Drain the grease from the beef in the strainer. Blot out the extra grease using a paper towel and set it aside.

3. Pour the soup and milk into a large mixing bowl and whisk them together.

4. Using a mixing spoon, stir in the hamburger and rice. Add a few dashes of salt and pepper.

5. Spray the baking pan with a non-stick spray.

6. Spoon all that into the baking pan and sprinkle the grated cheese over it.

7. Heat the oven up to 350°F (180°C).

8. Bake it for 30 minutes.

9. Place the casserole on the wire rack and let it cool for a few minutes before serving.

NOTE! *Add more variety if you want. For example, add any or all of these: a cup of corn niblets, a cup of peas, a cup of chopped carrots, 10 oz. (284 mL) of spinach, or a cup of onions.*

SOFT TACOS

TACO STUFF

1 lb. (500 g) ground beef, taco mix & 12 shells (store-bought),
1 1/2 cups grated Cheddar cheese, 3 chopped spring onions,
1 diced tomato, shredded lettuce, sour cream, salsa (store-bought)

THINGS YOU'LL NEED

frying pan, stirring fork, various bowls, cheese grater,
chopping knife, cutting board, spoon

1. Brown the ground beef in the frying pan over medium-high heat.

2. When the meat is all browned, add the prepared taco mix and stir it in with a fork. (Most taco mix recipes call for you to pre-mix them in water.)

3. Simmer for the time indicated on the package and stir it occasionally.

4. Grate the Cheddar into its own bowl.

5. On the cutting board, chop the spring onions and throw them into another bowl.

6. Dice the tomato and toss it into yet another bowl.

7. Shred the lettuce. Start with about a cup's worth. You can always shred more. Throw that into yet another bowl – a lot bowls so far. It's not over.

8. Spoon out the sour cream and salsa into 2 more small bowls.

9. Put the beef into –gosh yes – another bowl.

10. Microwave the taco shells for about 15 to 30 seconds at medium-high power.

NOTE! *This could be a night for bowling – get it? Uhhh, never mind.*

SOFT TACO LASGANA

TACO STUFF

1 lb. (500 g) beef, taco mix & 12 shells (store-bought), 6 chopped spring onions, 2 diced tomatoes, 1 1/2 cups grated Cheddar cheese

THINGS YOU'LL NEED

frying pan, chopping knife, cutting board, cheese grater, bowl, small casserole dish

1. Brown the meat in the pan (as you did in the SOFT TACOS recipe).

2. Chop the spring onions, dice the tomatoes, and leave them on the cutting board.

3. Grate the Cheddar into a bowl.

4. Layer 3 taco shells along the bottom of the casserole dish. They may overlap and not fit perfectly. Who cares …

5. Spread 1/3 of the meat over the shells.

6. Sprinkle 1/3 of the onions, tomatoes and cheese over the meat.

7. Add a second layer of taco shells and do the same drill with the toppings.

8. Add a third layer, same drill.

9. Top the whole thing with the last 3 taco shells.

10. Add lots of cheese on top. Grate more if you need to.

11. Bake the thing for 30 minutes at 350°F (180°C).

60

ANY PAN-FRIED STEAK

STEAK STUFF
any steak, 1 tsp. cooking oil, 1 tbsp. butter

THINGS YOU'LL NEED
cast iron frying pan or griddle pan, sauce brush, tongs or turner

1. Drop 1 tsp. of oil in the pan over medium-high heat.

2. Brush the butter on the steak.

3. Sear one side of the steak at high heat for 30 seconds, then, using the tongs or turner, flip it over and start cooking it for the specified time count according to the chart in this section (pg. 62). Remember to cook the thicker steaks at a medium heat.

4. Do not add too many steaks to the pan at one time. This drops the oil temperature, which can result in the grease being absorbed into the food.

NOTE! *Use a pan that conducts heat well, like cast iron. A thin, poorly conducting pan can have hot spots and burn foods. If you use a griddle pan, you do not have to use cooking oil.*

ABOUT HOW LONG TO FRY THE STEAK?

The following time guidelines are simply that – *guidelines* for a steak done **medium** with abit of pink. You'll have to go through some trial and error. I suggest you use a **medium-high** setting for thicker steaks, and **medium** for the even thicker slabs, simply because they take more time. High heats are used with thinner steaks.

NOTE! *¼ inch = .64 cm, ½ inch = 1.3 cm, ¾ inch = 1.9 cm, 1 inch = 2.5 cm, 1½ inch = 4 cm.*
Thank goodness we don't use metric time.

BEEF CUT	THICKNESS	TOTAL COOKING TIME TURN HALFWAY THROUGH
eye of round	½"	4 minutes
chuck top blade	½"	4 minutes
round tip	¼"	2 minutes
top sirloin	1"	10 to 14 minutes
ribeye	¾"	6 to 10 minutes
T-bone	¾ to 1¼"	8 to 10 minutes

62

ABOUT KNOWING
HOW DONE THE STEAK IS

The truth is, every stove, pan and steak is different. The best way to know if your steak is done the way you like it is to check the temperature.

Thermometer readings should be:

very rare	120-130°F (49-54°C)
rare	140°F (60°C)
medium-rare	145°F (63°C)
medium	155-160°F (68-71°C)
medium well	165°F (73°C)
well done	170°F (77°C)

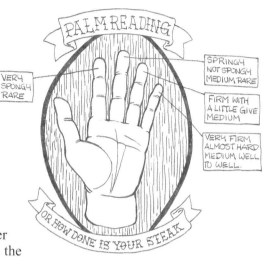

PALM READING

VERY SPONGY RARE

SPRINGY NOT SPONGY MEDIUM RARE

FIRM WITH A LITTLE GIVE MEDIUM

VERY FIRM ALMOST HARD MEDIUM WELL TO WELL.

OR HOW DONE IS YOUR STEAK

Another way to determine how done your steak is the FINGER TOUCH comparison test. The idea is to touch and lightly press your thumb tip with the tip of each of the index finger, the finger you use to show your feelings for other drivers, the fourth finger (ring finger) and the pinky.

(Or you can use the "This Little Piggy" nursery rhyme to identify your fingers.)

Then, with the other hand, press the hand muscle just below the thumb – the round, thick, part of the palm marked 'X' in the diagram. Here's how you figure out where your steak is at.

FINGER COMBO	HOW PALM FEELS	STEAK EQUIVALENT
touch thumb to index	very spongy	rare
touch thumb to 3rd finger	springy, not spongy	medium rare
touch thumb to 4th finger	firm, with a little give	medium
touch thumb to pinky	very firm, almost hard	medium well to well

Now, touch your steak and compare, using the additional guidelines below.

rare	meat gives easily when touched; no juices appear on surface.
medium	meat feels firm but springy; juices begin to appear on the surface.
well-done	meat is covered with juices and does not yield to pressure.

63

PASTA PASTA FASTA IF YOU PLEASE

Let's face it. Cooking with pasta is a challenge. What pasta do you choose? How do you measure the amount you need for a meal? How much water do you need to cook it? How do you know when the pasta is ready?. The good news is, you can always refrigerate left over pasta and reheat it in the microwave at medium power for 1 to 1½ minutes for lunch or dinner. Pasta can be an easy way to make a dinner if you follow my guidelines. Once you've figured out the pasta, the rest is easy. You just add stuff – like meatballs, sauces, or sliced ham – whatever you think will work with pasta – and it usually does.

ABOUT QUANTITIES
OF PASTA, WATER, SALT & OIL

According to *them* (unnamed experts), you need a gallon (4 quarts, 3.8 litres, or 16 cups) of water, 1 tbsp. of salt and 2 tbsp. of oil (or butter) for every pound (16 ounces, 500 grams) of pasta. You might benefit from having a little weigh scale for the pasta. But if you don't, the National Pasta Association offers you this guide: 2 oz. (55 g) of long pasta shapes, like spaghetti and linguini = a bunch in the diameter of a quarter. So you need 8 bunches for 4 people. The average amount of pasta a person eats at a main meal is equal to 4 oz. (approx 113 grams) of dry pasta. So if you're making a dinner for 4 people, you need 1 pound (500 grams) of dry pasta, which will require 16 cups of water. Here's a chart for other amounts.

AMOUNT OF PASTA	WATER	SALT	OIL/BUTTER/MARGARINE
24 oz. (680 g) (6 cups)	28 cups	4 tsp.	3 tbsp.
20 oz. (567 g) (5 cups)	24 cups	1 tbsp.	2 tbsp.
16 oz. (500 g) (4 cups)	16 cups	1 tbsp.	2 tbsp.
12 oz. (340 g) (3 cups)	16 cups	2 tsp.	2 tbsp.
10 oz. (283 g) (2½ cups)	8 cups	1½ tsp.	1 tbsp.
6 oz. (170 g) (1½ cups)	8 cups	1 tsp.	1 tbsp.
4 oz. (113 g) (1 cup)	8 cups	¾ tsp.	2 tsp.

4 ounces (113 g) of uncooked pasta (1 cup dried pasta) equals 2½ cups cooked elbow macaroni, shells, rotini, wheels, or penne. 4 ounces of uncooked or a 1" diameter bunch of dry pasta will equal 2 cups cooked spaghetti, angel hair, vermicelli, or linguine.

ABOUT THE TYPE OF PASTA TO CHOOSE

To go with pasta salads	macaroni, penne, fusilli, rotini
To go with heavy sauces	linguine, fettuccine, fusilli
To go with light, smooth sauces	spaghetti, vermicelli
To go with cream or butter sauces	spaghetti, fettuccine, penne
To go in dishes with chunky, bite-sized ingredients	macaroni, penne, fusilli, rigatoni rotini
To go in baked casseroles	macaroni, penne, fusilli rigatoni

ABOUT KNOWING IF IT'S READY

Properly cooked pasta is "al dente" (al DEN tay - Italian for "to the tooth"). What that means is the pasta is tender, yet still slightly chewy and resilient. If you bite it just before the full cooking time indicated on the package, you can see how much of the centre of the pasta is white (versus that darker, off-white, cooked color). You want to see just a little bit of white or whiter pasta inside. It will taste quite gummy if you have overcooked it. (Or, you accidentally dropped your gum into the pot.) One pound (500 g) of pasta takes about 8 to minutes to cook.

NOTE! *To keep the pasta firm and not sticky, add the salt when the water come to a boil, not before. If you use plenty of water, you don't necessarily have to use oil.*

CULPEPPER'S PASTA IN A HURRY

STUFF TO HURRY WITH

4 to 6 garlic cloves skinned & chopped, 16 cups water,
1 tbsp. salt, 2 tbsp. oil, 1/2 cup extra virgin olive oil,
1 lb. (500 g, 4 cups) pasta (any pasta),
1/2 cup chopped fresh parsley, seasoned salt & freshly ground pepper,
your favorite pasta sauce (store-bought)

THINGS YOU'LL NEED

chopping knife, cutting board, large pot, heavy saucepan,
pepper grinder, strainer, bowl, stirring spoon

1. Remove the skin from the garlic cloves. Then, chop them on the cutting board.

2. Heat the water in the large pot. When it boils, throw in the salt and oil.

3. Slowly drop in the pasta (not too fast or you'll get an ugly, foaming overflow). Stir it occasionally and check it after 8 minutes

4. In a separate, heavy saucepan, heat the olive oil and garlic over a medium heat until the garlic begins to turn pale gold.

5. Take the saucepan off the stove and toss in 3/4 of the parsley.

6. Add the seasoned salt and ground pepper to taste.

7. Back to the pasta. When it's done, drain the pasta in the strainer and rinse it with cold water.

8. Combine the pasta with the sauce in a bowl and stir it around until the pasta is coated.

9. Throw in the rest of the parsley.

NOTE! *Add anything to this dish: sauces, vegetables, meats, cheese – consider this the ultimate pasta-launching platform. My Kids sprinkle Parmesan cheese on top and have at her.*

HOMEMADE MAC AND CHEESE

MAC AND CHEESE STUFF

20 ounces (567 g, 5 cups) macaroni, 24 cups water, 2 tbsp. oil,
1 tbsp. salt, 12 cheese slices, 1/2 cup ketchup

THINGS YOU'LL NEED

large pot, strainer, casserole dish, stirring spoon

1. Fill the pot with water. Bring it to a boil. Add the salt and oil.

2. Slowly drop in the macaroni and cook it for about 10 minutes.

3. Check the macaroni to be sure it is "al dente". Drain the water from the macaroni using the strainer. **NOTE!** *Review the "ABOUT KNOWING IF IT'S READY" on page 65.*

4. Pour half the macaroni into the casserole dish.

5. Put half the cheese slices and half the ketchup on top. Do not stir anything yet.

6. Put the other half of the macaroni, cheese slices and ketchup on top of the first load. No stirring yet.

7. Bake the macaroni in an oven at 350°F (180°C) for 20 minutes or until the cheese is completely melted.

8. Take the casserole dish out of the oven.

9. Now you can stir everything, working in the cheese and the ketchup.

NOTE! *If you want the mixture to be a little more moist, add milk into the mix before baking. You can also throw in pieces of ham, pre-cooked bacon or sliced hot dog sausages.*

67

EZY SPAGHETTI FOR 4

SPAGHETTI STUFF
24 cups water, 2 tbsp. oil, 1 tbsp. salt,
20 oz. (567 g, five 1-inch bunches) spaghetti
24 oz. (710 mL) spaghetti sauce (store-bought), French bread,
grated Parmesan and Cheddar cheese (store-bought)

THINGS YOU'LL NEED
large pot, microwave-safe bowl, paper towel, strainer, stirring spoon

1. In the large pot, boil the water. When things are bubbling, drop in the oil and salt.

2. Gently put the spaghetti into the pot. Too fast and it foams over. Stir it occasionally.

3. Fill the microwave-safe bowl with half the bottle of sauce.

4. When the spaghetti is getting close (check after 8 to 10 minutes), then microwave the spaghetti sauce for about 2 to 3 minutes at high power. Cover the bowl with a paper towel, so the sauce doesn't splatter inside the microwave. Wear gloves when you take the bowl out.

5. Empty the spaghetti into a strainer in the sink and rinse it with cold water. This will stop the cooking process. If you just drain the water without cooling the noodles, they will continue to cook because there is heat still in the noodles.

6. Serve the spaghetti with French bread (or any stick loaf) and let the family top things off on their own choices: Cheddar, Parmesan, sauce.

NOTE! There are a bazillion sauce recipes. Example: cut up some hot sausage, pre-cook it and then serve it on a separate plate. Add as much as you want to the spaghetti.

SIMPLY PASTA SALAD

SIMPLE STUFF

16 cups water, 2 tbsp. oil, 2 tsp. salt, 12 oz. (340 g, 3 cups) pasta,
(macaroni or a small shell pasta like "fiori", which looks like a wheel,
"fusilli", which looks like a twisted rope, "rotini", which looks like a spiral
shape), 2 cups chopped veggies (onions, celery, carrots), 1/2 cup oil-based
Italian dressing

THINGS YOU'LL NEED

pot, strainer, bowl with lid, chopping knife, cutting board, mixing spoon

1. Simply bring the water to a boil. Drop in the oil and salt.

2. Simply put the pasta into the pot and cook it for 10 minutes.

3. Simply drain the pasta in the strainer and rinse it with cold water.

4. Simply transfer the pasta to a bowl.

5. On the cutting board, simply chop the veggies and mix them in with the pasta in the bowl.

6. Simply pour the dressing into the mix and stir it up.

7. Simply put the bowl in the fridge, cover it with the lid and leave it for about an hour to chill. Overnight is even better.

NOTE! *You can use other oil-based salad dressings. Simply add things like bacon bits, chopped ham, chopped chicken, and chopped cheese.*

69

SIMPLY CHICKEN SALAD

SIMPLE STUFF

2 chopped hard boil eggs, 2 or 3 boneless chicken breasts, melted butter,
3/4 cup sliced celery, 1/2 small onion, 1 tsp. lemon juice,
1/2 cup mayonnaise, 1/4 tsp. salt

THINGS YOU'LL NEED

pot, sauce brush, baking sheet, chopping knife, cutting board, bowl, mixing spoon

1. Simply hard boil the eggs. (See pg. 17.)

2. Simply heat the oven to 350°F (180°C).

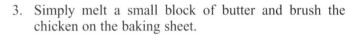

3. Simply melt a small block of butter and brush the chicken on the baking sheet.

4. Simply shove it into the oven, uncovered, for 1 hour. Make sure the chicken meat is fully white inside.

5. On the cutting board, simply chop the eggs, slice the celery, and cut the onion. Toss everything into the bowl.

6. Simply stir in the lemon juice and mayonnaise and then toss in a couple of dashes of salt.

7. When the chicken is ready, simply cut it into cubes throw it into the bowl.

8. Toss it. (And I don't mean to simply throw it away.)

NOTE! You can make this salad with leftover ham, which can also be cubed. Simply add chopped cheese. Throw in dry Chinese noodles (from those quickie soup packs) to give it a crunch.

THE HUBBUBB ABOUT SPUDS

The term "spud" comes from the 14th century tool used to dig holes in the soil prior to planting potatoes. It's amazing what I've learned about potatoes. They're, perhaps, the most versatile food on the planet. So, here is everything I feel most Dads need to know, from the types to the cooking methods, including baking, boiling, and nuking.

TYPES OF POTATOES

VARIETY	COOKING METHOD
russets	bake, mash, French fry
whites, yellows	all-purpose
reds	boil

1¼ pounds (567 g) or 3 medium potatoes equals 3 cups chopped or sliced raw potatoes or 2 to 3 cups cooked mashed potatoes. An average serving is about 1 potato per person. If the potatoes are smaller, make it 2 potatoes per person.

STORING POTATOES

Keep them in the dark. (Don't tell 'em anything.) DO NOT refrigerate. DO NOT freeze. HANDLE them carefully. Potatoes can bruise. DO NOT wash potatoes until you're ready to peel or prepare them.

PREPARATION

Wash them well in warm running water and scrub them with a clean vegetable brush. Don't break the skin. Scrub new potatoes gently because their skin is tender and can tear easily (like yours). Potatoes can be arranged flat in dish racks and run through the dishwasher WITHOUT detergent. Trim off any sprouts and peel away any green, tinged portion. Unless the recipe tells you otherwise, cook them with the peels on.

OVEN VS NUKE

They both work. I have recipes for both. On the following pages, the first set is oven-based; the second set is for the nuke machine.

OVEN BAKED POTATOES

STUFF
6 to 9 russet potatoes, cooking oil

THINGS YOU'LL NEED
scrubbing brush, baking sheet, fork, thermometer if you want to be scientific

1. Scrub 'em gently.
2. Rub each potato lightly with cooking oil. (Okay, massage is over.)
3. Pierce each potato several times with a fork so steam can escape.
4. Arrange them in an even layer on a baking sheet for easier handling.
5. Bake 6 to 9 potatoes in the oven between 1 hour and 1¼ hours at 350°F (180°C).

NOTE! A baked potato is fully cooked when its internal temperature reaches 210°F (99°C).

BOILED POTATOES

STUFF
all potato varieties, butter, dill,
salt (3 tbsp. for every 2 pounds/1 kg or about 6 medium potatoes)

THINGS YOU'LL NEED
peeler, slicing knife, cutting board, large pot, fork

1. Peel them.
2. On the cutting board, cut the potatoes into quarters. Try to keep the pieces about the same size.
3. Put them in a large pot and cover them with cold water. The surface of the water should be about a half inch above the potatoes. (1.27 cm for you metric fanatics.)
4. Boil the water.
5. Toss in the salt. (Remember: 3 tbsp. for every 2 pounds/1 kg or roughly 6 medium potatoes.)
6. Reduce the heat and simmer the 'taters for about 20 to 30 minutes 'til they're tender. Use a fork to check the tenderness.
7. Add the butter and dill when you serve them.

NOTE! To check for tenderness, pierce the potato with a fork and lift it up. Let gravity be your answer. If the potato slips off easily, it's tender. If it slips off, hits the floor and comes apart, then you'll know you should have held your other hand (wearing an oven mitt) under the potato.

POTATO IMASHINATION

MASHED POTATO STUFF
2 lbs. (1 kg) potatoes, 1 cup milk, 2 tbsp. butter, salt & pepper

THINGS YOU'LL NEED
bowl, potato masher or electric beater

1. Follow the BOILED POTATOES recipe (pg. 72).
2. When they're done, put the cooked potatoes into a bowl.
4. Stir in the milk and butter.
5. Mash the suckers. Or blend patiently.
6. Toss in dashes of salt and pepper to taste.

NOTE! Add a cheese spread, cream cheese, onions, Worcestershire sauce, hot English mustard, turnips, parsnips – use your imashination.

NUKED BAKED POTATOES

STUFF
russet potatoes

THINGS YOU'LL NEED
scrub brush, fork, paper towel

1. Scrub the potatoes gently.
2. Pierce them with a fork all around.
3. Wrap each potato in paper towel.
4. Place them end-to-end in a circle in the microwave with about a 1-inch (2.54 cm) space between each potato. Don't stack them in layers. It's like the circle of covered wagons you see in an old Western adventure.
5. Nuke them at HIGH power. Cooking times will vary with the size of the potato and the power of the oven.
6. About halfway through the cooking time, turn the potatoes over and change their position.

NOTE! Based on nuking an 8 oz. (250 g) potato in a 1000-watt oven, 1 potato will take 5 minutes, 2 potatoes 7 to 8 minutes, and 4 potatoes 13 to 15 minutes.

73

NUKED VEGGIES

VEGGIE STUFF
peas, corn niblets, green beans, broccoli, carrots, leafy veggies

THINGS YOU'LL NEED
microwave-safe containers, microwave-safe plastic wrap, paper towel

VEGGIES	WATER	COOKING TIME
peas, corn niblets	2 to 4 tbsp. per lb. (500 g)	10 min per lb. (500 g)
green beans, broccoli	2 to 4 tbsp. per lb. (500 g)	10 min per lb. (500 g)
carrots	1/3 cup per lb. (500 g)	10 to 12 min per lb. (500 g)
leafy vegetables like spinach	the water remaining on the leaves from rinsing is enough	4 to 6 min

1. Most veggies are best served tender-crisp. So, nuke them at high power.

2. When nuking veggies in a microwave-safe bowl or dish, cover the bowl or dish with a good quality microwave-safe plastic wrap or paper towel. Poke a couple of small holes in the wrap or towel to allow the steam to escape.

NOTE! To determine if a dish is microwave-safe, put the empty dish in the microwave with a cup of water. Nuke it on high (full power) for 1 minute. If the empty dish is warm or hot, don't use it. If the empty dish is cool and the water is hot, this dish is safe to use. A dish that becomes hot absorbs energy and will lengthen the cooking time or could break during the cooking process.

NUKED CORN HUSKS

CORN STUFF
fresh corn – leave the husk on (that's the outside leafy jacket)

THINGS YOU'LL NEED
paper towel

1. You don't have to husk fresh corn before cooking. (Meaning, you don't have to take off the outer leafy jacket.)

2. Pull back the husks just enough to remove any of the dry brown silk, the stringy stuff.

3. Close the husks back up.

4. Rinse the ears. (I'm referring to the corn, of course.)

5. Put the ears on a paper towel in the microwave. Arrange them like spokes on a wheel, with the narrow end of the ears facing the center of the oven.

6. Nuke 4 ears of corn for 4 to 5 minutes at high power.

7. Turn the ears over and nuke them for an additional 4 to 5 minutes.

8. Take the ears out of the microwave oven and carefully pull back and remove the husks and the silk. It will come off easily from the cooked corn.

BEST MICROWAVE POWER LEVELS FOR FOOD

HIGH POWER (100%): ground meats, chicken, turkey, seafood, bacon, fruits, vegetables, water-based soups and casseroles, pasta, reheating bread products.

MEDIUM-HIGH POWER (70%): rib roasts, foods containing cheese, cream-based soups and casseroles, reheating leftovers.

MEDIUM POWER (50%): ham, pork strips, spareribs, stew, eye or round roast, eggs, custards, softening cream cheese, melting chocolate.

MEDIUM-LOW POWER (30%): beef pot roasts, pork roasts and chops, lamb, simmering foods, rice, cereal, defrosting.

LOW POWER (10%): defrosting large roasts or turkeys, keeping foods warm, proofing yeast dough.

STANDING TIME: food cooks about 20% more after the microwave shuts off.

75

DESSERTS

I'm real lazy when it comes to desserts. So these recipes are for Dads like me. Wherever possible, use sugar substitutes that nutritionists will endorse, a reality that changes like the wind everyday. Look for low fat products, products containing no trans fat – and after all is said and done, a little something sweet every once in a while is not a sin and won't kill anyone.

OH SO SWEET BANANAS

STUFF

those 4 bananas that never seem to get eaten and are very ripe,
1 1/2 tbsp. butter, 4 tbsp. brown sugar, vanilla ice cream

THINGS YOU'LL NEED

saucepan, slicing knife, cutting board, spoon, turner,
ice cream scoop, serving bowls

1. Peel the bananas. On the cutting board, slice the bananas in half, length-wise, and then once across (kinda' like quartering a banana).

2. Melt the butter in the pan over medium heat.

3. Spoon the brown sugar into the pan and mix it with the butter.

4. Gently place the banana pieces into the pan. Use a spoon to cover them with the sauce.

5. Every once in a while, turn the bananas over, stirring the brown sugar-butter sauce and bathing the bananas in them.

6. After 10 minutes, spoon out the bananas into the serving bowls (careful, they're soft).

7. Drop one or 2 small scoops of vanilla ice cream on top and let the ice cream melt a little. Plan to go on a diet.

PUDDING PIE

PIE STUFF

4 oz. (113 g) instant pudding mix (store-bought),
8-inch (20 cm) piecrust (comes in its own dish), 1 cup milk, whipping cream

THINGS YOU'LL NEED

mixing bowl, mixing spoon

1. In the bowl, blend together the pudding mix, the whipping cream and the milk. Set it aside.

2. Put the piecrust into the oven. (Leave it in its dish.)

3. Bake the piecrust at 425°F (220°C) for 8 to 20 minutes or according to the package instructions.

4. Take the piecrust out of the oven. Let it cool.

5. Spoon the pudding into the piecrust and top it with more whipping cream. Lick the bowl. Lick the spoon. Lick your fingers.

6. Refrigerate the pie for 45 minutes to an hour.

NOTE! *Sprinkle chocolate flakes or cinnamon on top. Add pieces of fruit, like strawberries.*

FUN-DO

FUN-DO STUFF
instant pudding mixes (store-bought) (chocolate, vanilla, strawberry),
fruits you can poke (strawberries, grapes, harder bananas)

THINGS YOU'LL NEED
1 bowl for EACH pudding, slicing knife, cutting board,
forks or fondue spears, serving plate with dividers

1. Make the puddings according to the package directions. You want to end up with 3 full bowls – one bowl for each pudding flavour.

2. Put them in the fridge and let them cool.

3. On the cutting board, slice the strawberries in half and the bananas into bite-sized pieces. Clean the grapes.

4. Put the fruit on a serving plate – the ones that have those little dividers. If you don't have one, just throw them all on the same plate.

5. Bring out the pudding bowls.

6. Hand the weapons to your Kids and dip away.

CARAMALLOWS

2 cups rice crispies type cereal, 12 marshmallows,
1/2 cup caramel ice cream topping

THINGS YOU'LL NEED
bowl, wooden kabob skewer sticks, spoon, waxed paper, plate

1. Pour the rice crispies into a soup bowl or snack bowl. Fill it at least half way.
1. Put a marshmallow on a stick.
2. Smother the mallow in the caramel topping using a spoon.
3. Roll the coated mallow in the crispies.
4. Put 'em on waxed paper on a plate and stick 'em in the fridge.

NOTE! *Do the same with a chocolate topping.*

FAST FUDGE

FAST STUFF
12 oz. (354 mL) can sweetened condensed milk,
12 oz. (340 g) package of semi-sweet chocolate chips

THINGS YOU'LL NEED
microwave-safe bowl, paper towel, stirring spoon, greased pan

1. Pour the milk into the bowl and drop in the chocolate chips.
2. Microwave the mixture for 3 minutes at medium power. Cover the bowl with a paper towel.
3. Every minute, stir the mixture with a spoon. You want to get it thick and smooth.
4. Pour the mixture into the pan and let it cool.

NOTE! *You can also melt the mixture in a saucepan over low heat on the stove.*

MILK SHAKES

SHAKE STUFF

2 oz. (59 mL) syrup (vanilla, strawberry, chocolate), 1 oz. (29 mL) milk,
4 scoops ice cream (vanilla, strawberry, chocolate)

THINGS YOU'LL NEED

spoon, ice cream scoop, blender

1. Spoon and scoop all the ingredients into a blender. The syrup and the ice cream should be the same flavour.

2. Blend everything together at high speed until it looks creamy.

2. Add a little more milk or ice cream until you get the thickness you want.

NOTE! *Toss fruit, like thawed strawberries, into either the vanilla or strawberry milkshake.*

GROOVY SMOOTHY

GROOVY STUFF

2 cups crushed ice, 2 cups fresh fruit, 1 cup vanilla yogurt,
1 tsp. powdered milk, 2 scoops vanilla ice cream

THINGS YOU'LL NEED

spoon, ice cream scoop, blender

1. Spoon and scoop all the ingredients into a blender and mix the crap out of it.

HOW TO SET THE TABLE

Sure, there's a proper way to do it, but the objective is to get your Kids involved. You may eventually come up with your own placement plan, but it's time well spent, and Kids love putting things together.

Of course, you don't have to do this for every meal. It ends up being a great help to Dad and a chance to talk about things while the activity is taking place.

81

THINGS YOU'LL NEED
patience

LUNCH

As I understand it, the basic method is to set things up so you use utensils from the outside in.

(above the plate. left to right): bread & butter plate, butter knife, wine/water glass
(plate row. left to right): napkin, salad fork, dinner fork, salad plate, plate, dinner knife

FORMAL DINNER

The same principle applies to dinner, but there's lots more stuff.

(above the plate. left to right): dessert fork & spoon, water/wine glasses.
(plate row: left to right): fish fork, dinner fork, salad fork, napkin, rim soup plate, plate,
salad knife, dinner knife, fish knife, soup spoon.

SNACK ATTACKS

Snacks sell in excess of 60 billion dollars a year, almost as much as Bill Gates is worth – or is he worth more? Does Bill eat chips? It has become a science for snack makers who are focused on the whims and taste buds of snackers everywhere. Somewhere between taste and nutrition, food scientists and marketers have concocted and packaged the thousands of snacks we consume every day, several times a day.

According to CNN and the Mayo Clinic, 25 percent of our Kid's daily energy intake comes from snacks. The report also states that, "Young children actually need snacks. Their stomachs are small, so they often can't get all the nutrients they need in a day through meals alone." What's the recommendation? You need a good snack plan.

There are several people in history to either blame or celebrate for the introduction and proliferation of snacks. There are several billion people consuming the fruits of their labor, perpetuating their legacies.

POPCORN

In the early 16th century, Cortes invaded Mexico. The Aztecs he met were wearing something called "pisancalla" as decorations for ceremonial headdresses and necklaces. "Pisancalla", as it turned out, was popped corn, an important food for the Aztec Indians. It's uncertain who came up with the idea to put butter on it.

CHOCOLATE BARS

Although Christopher Columbus was given his first drink of "xocoatl" (chocolate) on his fourth voyage to America in 1502, it wasn't until 1674 when a London coffeehouse sold the first solid chocolate in a stick form. The chocolate bar, as we know it today, didn't appear until 1900 when Milton S. Hershey introduced the Milk Chocolate Bar.

POTATO CHIPS

Thomas Jefferson first tasted French fries in Europe, where they had become extremely popular. He brought the concept back with him and it was the start of a new revolution in America (and everyone thought the revolution started with tea).

Decades later, in 1853, George Crum, a Native American chef employed at a Saratoga Springs resort in New York, received a complaint from a customer about his fries. Apparently, they were too thick. So, Crum served a thinner batch, but the customer still wasn't satisfied. Crum was ready to slice up the customer, but, instead, he sliced the potatoes as thin as possible. The customer couldn't get enough of them and the "potato chip" became the newest sensation.

It wasn't until the 1920s, when Herman Lay started selling them from the trunk of his car, that the chip went from being a local dish to a popular snack.

PRETZELS

Somewhere in Europe, around 600 BC, a monk was trying to figure out what to do with the dough that was leftover after making unleavened bread for Lent. He experimented with shapes and came up with a design that emulated the way people in those days prayed – with their hands across their chests. The monk called it "pretiola" , which, in Latin, means "little reward".

TIPS TO SNACKS

1. **Use fruits rather than fruit juices that are higher in calories**. That's why I have a bowl on the kitchen table with apples, pears and oranges. Two glasses of juice are plenty. No more than 12 oz. (354 mL) a day is recommended.

2. **Tell the Kids to brush their teeth after consuming snacks**. Gooey snacks are loaded with sugar and continue to cause damage to teeth all day long.

3. **Cut down on the TV-related snack time**. Avoid raising couch potatoes. Sit the Kids down at the table for a more formal snack, like crackers and cheese.

4. **When you offer snack choices, stick to a category**. In other words, give them a choice between an orange and an apple, rather than between fruits or chips. Keep the choices similar. If they switch categories on you, follow the same drill.

5. **Offer milk as a snack**. Remember, milk is a food. Milk and cookies are a small dinner.

6. **Turn down snack requests gently – but firmly – within 90 minutes of a major meal**. For example, if you eat at 6:00, give them a good snack by no later than 4:30.

7. **Do a diagnosis when they ask for a snack**. Is it salt they crave? Something sweet or tangy? Then take it from there. Cookies are sweet, but so are granola bars and cereals.

8. **Keep an open mind about low-fat snacks**. For the longest time, I avoided the low-fat thing, thinking that it sacrificed on taste. To my surprise, low-fat products on the market today actually taste good.

9. **Reacquaint your Kids and yourself with water**. There are flavored waters out there that rock and my Kids love 'em.

10. **Strike a balance**. It's not about always avoiding snacks, especially those that get bad editorials. I'm amazed at how quickly Kids will follow my lead. They will eat yogurt. They *will* drink water. I'd keep going, but I feel like a snack.

CELERY LOG

LOG STUFF
celery sticks, spreads (cheese spread, cream cheese),
toppings (raisins, ham, cooked bacon)

THINGS YOU'LL NEED
slicing knife, cutting board, spoon

1. Wash the celery.
2. On the cutting board, slice the celery sticks into pieces of shorter length.
3. Spoon the spread of your choice into the groove of the celery stick.
4. If you're using pepperoni, ham and bacon, slice them into small pieces.
5. Press the topping or toppings of your choice into the spread.

NOTE! Use one topping, or combine a couple. Generally, raisins work best alone. (They have their raisins for it, I guess.)

WHOLY DONUT HOLES

WHOLE STUFF
4 cans ready-to-bake biscuit dough (store-bought),
powdered sugar, 1 cup cooking oil

THINGS YOU'LL NEED
round plastic container with a lid, pot, knife, cutting board, tongs,
paper towel

1. Put enough powdered sugar in the plastic container so you can coat the balls you make later.
2. Heat up the oil in a pot over medium-high heat.
3. On the cutting board, cut the dough up and make small balls out of the pieces.
4. When the oil is hot, use the tongs to put the balls gently into the pot (as many as the pot will handle). (You might want to wear oven mits as a precaution.)
5. Cook the balls until they're golden brown.
6. Using the tongs, take them out of the pot and dab off the oil with a paper towel.
7. Place one ball at a time in the container with the powdered sugar and shake it while listening to your favorite rumba tune.

NOTE! Add cinnamon to the powdered sugar. Nummy!

ADAM'S APPLE

ADAM'S STUFF

4 medium-sized apples (in other words, not small ones),
1/2 cup instant non-fat dry milk, 1/2 cup peanut butter, 2 tbsp. raisins,
1/4 cup crushed cereal (just about any ready-to-eat cereal will do)

THINGS YOU'LL NEED

apple core tool, cutting board, mixing bowl, mixing spoon or popsicle stick

1. On the cutting board, cut out the core of the apple using the tool. You may want to use a knife to make the tunnel you created a little larger. Set the apples aside.

2. In the bowl, mix all the other stuff.

3. Now, take each apple and stuff the tunnel with your – well – stuffing. Use the popsicle stick as a stuffing tool.

4. You can either leave the apples whole, or slice them in half.

89

CRACKER STACKER

STACKER STUFF
square or round crackers (I like stone wheat), deli meats, sliced cheeses

THINGS YOU'LL NEED
2 plates, slicing knife, cutting board, vacuum cleaner

1. Lay out a bunch of crackers on one dish.
2. On the cutting board, slice the deli meats and cheeses into sizes that will fit on the crackers.
3. Lay out the meats and cheeses on a second plate.

NOTE! Tell the Kids to wash their hands before they start grabbing things. As an option, use small round buns. This is a good way to get rid of all those hamburger and hot dog buns, which mysteriously accumulate in the freezer.

FRUIT MALLOW PLATTER

PLATTER STUFF
1 jar marshmallow cream (store-bought), 8 oz. (250 g) cream cheese, fruits

THINGS YOU'LL NEED
microwave-safe container, mixing bowl, mixing fork,
slicing knife, cutting board, platter, forks

1. In the container, microwave the cream cheese at medium power for 45 to 60 seconds to soften it up. If it's not soft enough, do it again for 20 seconds.
2. In a bowl, use a fork to mix together the cream cheese and the marshmallow cream.
3. On the cutting board, slice the fruits into smaller pieces. You can also use whole grapes.
4. Set out the fruit and the dip on a platter. Hand out the forks.

NOTE! This works for lunches, too.

TRAIL MIX

MIX STUFF
a cereal Kids can grab with their fingers, raisins, assorted peanuts

THINGS YOU'LL NEED
mixing container with lid, zip-type bags

1. In the container, toss in a half cup of raisins and a half cup of peanuts for every cup of cereal.

2. Put the lid on the bowl and shake it, baby, shake it.

3. Scoop a cup of mix into separate bags.

NOTE! Add dried fruit. Kids seem to like dried banana pieces. If your Kids take this mix to school, instruct them to ask friends if they have an allergy to peanuts before offering any.

THE THRILL AND GRILL OF THE BBQ

By the end of the colonial period in America, roughly at the time of the American revolution in the late 18th century (the 1770's), the barbecue (BBQ) was a common thing. The origin of the word itself, "barbecue", is hotly debated. Some say it is a derivative of the West Indian term "barbacoa", which refers to a method of cooking meat slowly over hot coals.

Other word guys say the French phrase, "barbe a queue", meaning "from head to tail", is the origin. There are those who believe it came from a nineteenth century advertisement for a combination whiskey bar, beer hall, pool establishment famous for its roast pig, known as the BAR-BEER-CUE-PIG. S. Jonathan Bass, *How 'bout a Hand for the Hog': – The Enduring Nature of the Swine as a Cultural Symbol of the South*, Southern Culture, Vol. 1, No. 3, Spring 1995.

One thing is certain. Where there is a BBQ, there usually are a bar, beer, and a cue of people lining up to indulge.

The evolutions of BBQ equipment, accessories and recipes have led to a huge industry. There are over 3 billion BBQ events a year. Three out of four households in North America own a BBQ. Men commanding the sacred tong outnumber women by two to one.

So, brothers of the 'hood, it's twice as much about us.

My Kids are proud of my BBQ talents and often boast to others about my ability to BBQ a steak, turning it over only once in the specified number of minutes according to thickness.

My hamburgers are never dry coming off the grill. Hotdogs are evenly cooked. My garlic bread? Well, there should be hall of fame. In fact, there are several of them, quite unofficial, but I have yet to find the definitive temple of the flame and grill.

BBQ TIPS

1. **Use tin foil**. You can expand your BBQ menu to include veggies and fish using the stuff.

2. **Get a temperature gauge or thermometer** – unless you're psychic.

3. **Lightly oil the grill rather than the food**. This prevents meat from sticking to the grill.

4. **Grill leaner meats at lower heat**. Otherwise, life gets tough at the dining table.

5. **If you use a fork, you will be shot**. If you put a hole in a bucket of water, what happens?

6. **Don't use water sprayers to keep the flames down**. If you're using coals or briquets, a water sprayer will stir up the ashes. Ashes do not make a great BBQ sauce. When water hits fat, it spits back. If you're getting too many flames, you're leaking more juices than you should. To avoid excessive leaking, sear one side of your steak or filet for about 30 seconds at high heat and then turn it over to start the rest of the cooking process. In other words, searing helps seal juices in the meat. Searing doesn't mean shopping at Sears; it means to scorch or lightly burn.

7. **When you're finished BBQing, turn the gas or propane tank off first to allow the remaining gas in the hoses to be burned off**. Then turn the dials off on the BBQ. If you're using electricity, the oil companies hate you.

8. **Think safety, safety, safety** – especially with younger children around. Make it a habit to keep them at a distance when lighting the BBQ.

9. **Clean the grill before and after use**. If your scraper is missing, use crumpled tin foil.

10. **Make sure your Kids understand that BBQing is a rite of passage into manhood – even if you're a girl.**

HAMBURGER HAMSTORY

The word "hamburger" comes from Hamburg, Germany. The story is that Hamburgians served scraps of meat on a "Brötchen" – basically, a round bun. German immigrants then took the Hamburger to the US.

From there, the burger history in North America is subject to much debate. Some say that the first hamburgers were served in New Haven, Connecticut, at the "Louis' Lunch" san'wich shop, which was established in 1895 on Meadow Street in New Haven. Apparently, in 1900, Louis Lassen, the operator of Louis' Lunch, created a quick meal for a busy office worker by putting a broiled beef patty between two pieces of white toast.

McDonald's historians claim the inventor was Fletcher Davis of Athens, Texas, an unknown food vendor at the turn of the last century. He sold san'wichz of ground beef between two slices of bread at his lunch counter. Davis and his wife Ciddy, backed by local business people, took their san'wich to the St. Louis Fair in 1904. In 2006, the Texas State Legislature introduced Bill HCR-15, designating Athens as the "Original home of the hamburger".

The cheeseburger is said to have made its debut in 1924 and was created by grill chef, Lionel Sternberger, of The Rite Spot Restaurant in Pasadena, California.

BBQ FAQ CHART

In general, the heat guidelines are as follows: low = 300°F (150°C), medium = 500°F (260°C), high = 650°F (343°C). I bought myself one of those heat gauges you can stick right on the surface of the grill. I found that the heat on the grill is about 30 to 40 degrees higher than the gauge on the outside of the BBQ. So, if you're BBQ gauge is reading 400°F (200°C), it might be more like 440°F (227°C).

For thick meats, medium is the better heat, because it cooks the meat right through. At high heat, you'll dry out the meat. Below is a chart for the things I BBQ most. I always sear one side of anything for 30 seconds at high heat, then turn it over and drop the heat to the desired cooking temperature. With steaks, I turn them over only once (not including the turn after searing).

NOTE! *½ inch = 1.3 cm, ¾ inch = 2 cm, 1 inch = 2.5 cm.*

FOOD	SETTING	COOKING TIME
hamburger ¾ inch thick	medium	medium: 8 to 10 minutes well done: 10 to 15 minutes
frozen hamburger patties	low to medium	medium: 12 to 14 minutes
steak 1-inch thick	medium	rare: 4 to 6 minutes medium: 6 to 9 minutes well done: 9 to 12 minutes
steak 1-inch thick	high	rare: 3 to 5 minutes
pork chops ½ inch thick	medium	medium: 8 to 10 minutes well done: 15 to 20 minutes
boneless chicken breasts (halves)	medium	10 to 12 minutes
fish fillets 6 to 8 oz. 170 to 250 g	medium to high	8 to 12 minutes
whole baking potato in foil	medium	25 to 30 minutes

COUSIN KAREN CULPEPPER'S CRISPY HAMBURGERS

MEAT STUFF
1/2 lb. (250 g) extra lean ground beef

OTHER STUFF
1 egg, 1 cup saltine crackers, 6 dashes salt, 4 dashes seasoned salt,
6 dashes pepper, 4 dashes garlic powder, 1 tbsp. Lea Perrins sauce,
1/4 cup ketchup, BBQ sauce (optional), cheese slices (optional)

THINGS YOU'LL NEED
mixing bowl, mixing fork, zip-type bag, plate with parchment paper,
meat turner, sauce brush

1. In a bowl, mix all the ingredients, except the crackers.

2. Crush the crackers in a zip-type bag, then mix them with the meat.

3. Make your patties about 3 to 4 inches (7.6 cm to 10 cm) in diameter. Makes about 10 patties.

4. Using your finger, make a hole in the middle of the hamburger. The hole should be a bit larger than your pointing finger (the piggy who went to market).

5. Put them on the parchment paper on the plate.

6. Preheat the BBQ to high heat, about 600 to 650°F (316 to 343°C).

7. Sear one side of the burgers for about 1 minute, then turn them over.

8. Reduce the BBQ to medium heat (about 400°F/200°C) and grill the burgers for 5 minutes.

9. Turn the burgers over. Brush BBQ sauce on the top.

10. Grill them for another 5 minutes and turn again. Brush BBQ sauce on the top.

11. Grill them for yet for another 5 minutes and turn them over one last time. This is when you throw the cheese slice on top.

12. Grill the burgers for the last 5 minutes and you're done.

NOTE! Adding the egg adds 5 minutes to the cooking time for a total of 20 minutes. If you don't use an egg, you may want to reduce your grill time to around 15 minutes.

HOT DOG KABOB or HOT BOB KADOG

KABOB STUFF

all-beef or all-chicken wieners, tomatoes, green peppers, zucchini, BBQ sauce, hot dog buns

THINGS YOU'LL NEED

slicing knife, cutting board, wooden or metal skewers, tin foil, tongs, sauce brush

1. On the cutting board, slice the wieners into 1-inch (2.5 cm) lengths.
2. Slice the veggies into pieces that can be skewered.
3. Put the pieces on the skewer. Alternate a piece of wiener with a veggie. If the skewer is wooden, then wrap the ends in foil. You can also soak the wooden skewers in water for about 5 minutes before using them. If they're metal, they absorb heat, so protect your hands.
4. Heat the BBQ up to medium and place the kabobs on the grill.
5. Turn the kabobs frequently using the tongs.
6. Brush BBQ sauce on them every once in a while.
7. When they're done (veggies might be a bit scorched at the ends), lay the kabobs in the buns. Remove the skewers.

BBQ, LETTUCE & TOMATO SAN'WICH

BLT STUFF

1 1/2 lb. (750 g) back bacon, 1/2 cup honey mustard, tomatoes, lettuce, onions, pickles, bread rolls

THINGS YOU'LL NEED

slicing knife, cutting board, plate, sauce brush, tongs

1. If the back bacon isn't already sliced, cut it into ¼-inch slices. You can always ask the person at your deli counter to do that for you when you're buying it. This back bacon is also known as "peameal" bacon.
2. On the cutting board, slice up the veggies and arrange all the fixings on a separate plate.
3. Heat the BBQ up to medium. Place the bacon slices on the grill and brush the sides with the honey mustard.
4. Cook the back bacon about 2 to 3 minutes per side. If it starts to look leathery, you've overcooked it. Use the tongs to turn the bacon.
5. Place the cooked slices on a separate plate. Let the Kids do the assembly work.

CHAPTER 2

PLAYING TOGETHER

SURVIVING THE FUN

For the longest time, I've felt guilty about not doing enough with my Kids. But as I've aged, like a cheap wine, I've realized that what the Kids really want has more to do with time spent together, rather than turning life into a Disneyland experience.

So, I started to worry a little less about what we were doing and focused more on taking the time to be together in a way that kept me engaged, too. There is nothing worse than doing something with your Kids when your mind or heart don't come along for the ride.

TIPS TO ACTIVITES

1. **Be honest with yourself**. For example, if you're not a morning person, don't force the issue and try to participate at a time when you simply don't feel like it. Instead, let your Kids know about this truth and politely ask them to do their own thing. If anything, become a master of suggestions.

2. **For Dads who are time-challenged, like single, weekend Dads, remind yourself that you're not an amusement park**. Guilt often drives single Dads to fill the weekend with so many activities that even the Kids are more stressed than impressed. Think of it this way. What does a normal weekend look like? There's nothing wrong with a normal weekend that includes homework, puttzing around in the yard, and doing the laundry. These are all normal activities and you can choose when to get your Kids involved.

3. **Get your Kids involved**. If you have a normal routine, which requires your time on a regular basis, such as cutting the lawn, washing the car (even at the car wash), or cleaning the garage, include the Kids, even if it's in a minor way. I'm always amazed at how much fun they discover on their own within an activity not recommended by most experts. It doesn't matter if the Kids actually help you accomplish anything. It's the time they spend around you, asking questions and learning. Believe it or not, you're teaching them about responsibility. My tweenager has spent hours hammering nails into a block of wood. He knows what he's building. I don't. Doesn't matter. He's learned how to handle a hammer and do something creative.

4. **Explore your community**. Money is always an issue. There are more free programs being developed every year, which are designed for Dads and Kids. My Kids love going to the library. While they participate in a library program, I check out the stuff I like. Everyone wins.

5. **Remember, eating together is an activity**. Ah yes, even the simple things …

6. **Learn about the games your Kids are playing**. It's one-on-one time well spent and it's okay if you're just a spectator. "Spectating" is an activity. It also helps you determine if what they're playing is appropriate. Video and computer games are addictive. Find out why.

7. **Explore the nature of your Kids' creativity**. Are they builders or role players? What kinds of games or activities do you see them gravitating to? What you learn will help you choose activities that can enrich both your lives.

8. **Take the time to do some things one-on-one**. Too often, Dads feel that the only worthwhile activities are the ones that involve everyone. Who made up that rule? Mom?

9. **Do things with them, which they think they hate to do**. My Dad made me hike up mountains. Guess what I remember fondly about my Dad? Hiking up mountains and enjoying the view, a view I would never have seen without his nagging me every step of the way. I still like to hike up mountains.

10. **Sometimes, be selfish**. Inside each of us is a Kid still wanting to play. What do you like to play or do? Sometimes, it's okay to be selfish. Whenever possible, involve your Kids, even if it's only to watch. They're great cheerleaders.

INDOOR ACTIVITIES

103

CARD GAMES
THE KING'S ROYAL RACE

You need 1 deck. Number of players: 3 to 4 people, ages 6 and up. One player must act as the "Master of the Race". Players take turns being the Master. The lowest number of players is three – 2 Racers and 1 Master. The highest number is four – 3 Racers and 1 Master.

1. In one vertical column, line up the cards of one suit from Ace to King (choose one of the suits for the column: hearts, diamonds, clubs or spades). The Ace is at the top and the King is at the bottom. If the playing surface is too small for one column, break it into 2 or 3 columns, allowing enough space in between for the racers.

2. Next to the Ace, place the King of each of the remaining 3 suits in a row across. These are the Racers. Their position next to the ace is the starting position. If there are only 2 players, then put down only 2 Kings and discard the remaining King.

3. Shuffle the remaining cards.

4. The Master holds up a card such that the other racers cannot see it.

5. The Racers guess the suit.

6. When any Racer correctly guesses the suit, the King advances to the next row. (To the 2, then the 3, then 4 – right through to the King).

7. The first Racer to get to the bottom of the column (or the King card position) wins the race.

8. If the card being guessed is an Ace, Queen or Jack, the correct guessers advance 2 rows.

OLD MAN

You need 1 deck. Number of players: 2 up to the entire family, friends, guests, party crashers, ages 4 and up.

1. Remove one of the Kings. Deal all the cards among the players.

2. In each player's turn, the player puts down any pairs in their hand. Even if there are 3 of a kind, only 2 can be put down.

3. Still in the same turn, the player presents their hand to the player on the left (presenting the back of the cards so the next player cannot see the cards).

4. The second player chooses a card and then takes their turn.

5. Play continues until one person is left with one card, which is the odd King or "Old Man".

NO FISH

You need 1 deck. Number of players: 2 up to the entire family, ages 6 and up.

1. Deal all the cards. There is no stockpile in this version.

2. In each turn, a player asks the player to the left for a card by rank; eg. "Do you have a '10'"?

3. If the next player has the "10", it is given to the player asking for it. If not, the player says "No fish."

4. If the first player is successful and gets the card asked for, that player continues, and may ask any player at the table for cards until a player says, "No fish."

5. When a player gets 4 of a kind, known as a "book", that player lays down the book.

6. The player with the most "books" wins.

CREATIVE ACTIVITIES
KITCHEN KREATIONS

THINGS YOU'LL NEED

interlocking pieces (like Lego™), containers, kitchen items

Video and computer games are taking Kids away from the more tactile activities. The best way to get your Kids actively engaged in the hands-on types of activities is to participate with them. After a while, they'll do it on their own, too.

1. Gather all the interlocking pieces in the house.

2. Divide them up into at least 3 categories, placing them in 3 different containers: structural pieces (the basic building blocks), wheels and wings, and special pieces (which can be anything else).

3. Each person then picks a small kitchen item or tool that is not breakable or potentially harmful (like a knife).

4. The objective is to create an object that uses the kitchen object and the pieces together.

NOTE! *Do a careful sweep of the floor for small pieces after the fact. Ever stepped on a small piece?*

TICKLE TRUNK BALLOON PEOPLE

THINGS YOU'LL NEED

balloons of all shapes, long straws or sticks, felt markers, clothes, tape, string, pins, newspapers stuffed into plastic bags

This is an activity that helps you weed through old clothes (and other things) to find new purpose for them. My tickle trunk has everything from old motorcycle helmets to capes. It's an endless source of entertainment. At Halloween, it can be a solution to the question, "What am I going to be this year?" My Kids and I have also created balloon people as Halloween decorations.

1. Go through every clothes closet and drawer, yours included, and choose clothing items that are no longer being used: pants, dresses, tops, shirts, hats, gloves – anything.

2. Blow up a balloon for each participant. Tie the balloon to a long straw or stick.

3. Give everybody a marker and direct them to draw a face on the round balloon.

OPTION! Use ping-pong balls with 2-sided tape to create eyes.

4. Use the newspapers stuffed in plastic bags to stuff the shirts or tops, arms and legs.

5. Attach the head assembly by taping the attached stick to the inside of the shirt or top.

6. Pin gloves to the cuffs of shirts or tops.

7. Name your character.

8. When you're ready to retire the balloon family, put all the clothes in a trunk – now known as the "tickle trunk".

NOTE! If you use recycling bags for the newspapers, then you can put them out for pickup after the balloon family has been retired.

BOX CASTLE – BIG & SMALL

THINGS YOU'LL NEED

boxes of all sizes, cardboard rolls, exacto knife, packing tape, felt markers

Boxes of all sizes are worth their empty weight in gold. If you happen to have large boxes (after that appliance purchase), you're in luck. Even if you don't, small boxes work like bricks. You can always source boxes from retail stores, such as grocery stores, liquor stores, appliance and hardware stores. Tissue boxes and the leftover cardboard rolls from wrapping paper and toilet paper can all be used as raw building materials.

1. Generally, a large box works best with the top flaps cut off. This means that the bottom of the cardboard box acts as the floor.

2. Cut the top of the wall to create the turrets. An option is to attach smaller boxes on the outside or use cardboard rolls to create 3-dimensional turrets.

3. To create the drawbridge, cut out a half-oval shaped door, leaving it hinged at the floorline. Attach the door and the adjoining wall using 2 strings. The idea is that the Kids can pull up the drawbridge from the inside of the castle.

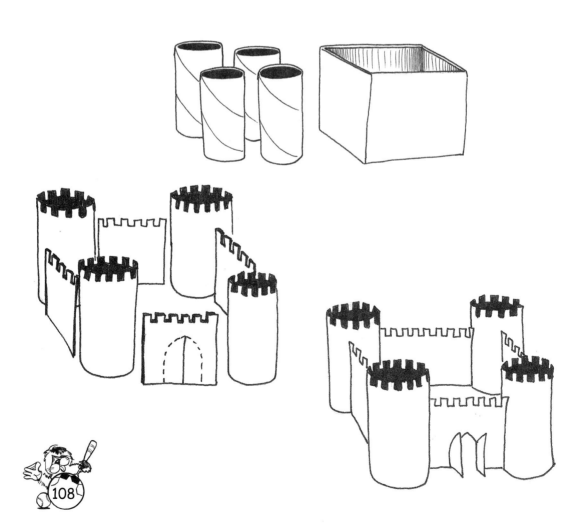

PAPER COLLAGE COMIX

Ever wonder what to do with all those old magazines, newspapers and flyers? On a rainy or cold day, this activity will keep Kids of all ages – and Dads – busy for hours. You can work together on the same piece or do your own thing. Whatever you choose to do, it doesn't have to make perfect sense. In fact, the stranger it is, the more laughs you'll enjoy. It makes for a great creative keepsake.

THINGS YOU'LL NEED
magazines, newspapers, flyers, stiff art-board or paper, scissors

1. Agree on a rough theme or storyline. Good versus evil. Search for discovery or invention. Fantasy quest. Things that move. Flowers and insects. Weird faces. Geometric shapes.

2. If you're creating a story, work with 4 layers: the background, the characters, the objects and the dialogue or narrative.

3. Start with the background. You can always add or change things with additional images.

4. Build your characters and give them objects.

5. Cut out words to make up dialogue. You can also create a narrative along the bottom of the page, rather than have the characters actually speak.

7. If there are several pages, bind them either with a plastic end-binder , which you can get in an office supply or art store. You can also use a 3-hole punch and put them into a 3-ring binder.

INTERNET COLLAGE COMIX

If you're hooked up to the Internet and have a printer, you can also grab pictures of anything from many sites, print them, and use them to make your collage. Now you can create multi-page stories using different images of the same person, which are easier to source online.

THINGS YOU'LL NEED

computer, internet connection, printer, some experience with computers & images

1. Create a folder called "Collage" on your computer. The easiest place to locate your folder is right on your desktop. (For you experienced types, it's your choice where you put the folder.)

2. Go on the Internet. Right click on any image you find on a website. The dialogue that appears will give you several options. Usually, you can choose either *Save target as …* or *Save picture as …* (If a dialogue box doesn't appear, you cannot select that image.)

3. Assuming a dialogue box has appeared, click on one of the options I mentioned. The next box that appears will offer you the opportunity to choose the location where you can save the picture. Find the location of your folder and save your picture there.

4. When you're finished collecting images, close down the Internet.

5. Open the folder containing all the images.

6. Double click on an image. Your computer should open it up automatically in your computer's resident imaging program. On my PC, when I click on an image, it automatically comes up in a "Windows Picture Viewer".

7. Usually, you will be able to choose to print the image by selecting a command from the tool-bar of your imaging program (mine has a little printer icon at the bottom of the viewer).

8. It may be that your selected image will print out smaller or larger. If you're not familiar with the process of resizing images using graphics programs, then don't beat yourself up. Get out the magazines, newspapers and scissors.

TISSUE BOX GUITAR

Add pots and pans to this, and you have a band.

THINGS YOU'LL NEED

tissue box, elastic bands, pencil, cardboard roll

1. Stretch the elastic band around the box.

2. Place a pencil under the elastic band on one side of the opening. This will lift the rubber bands off the surface so they can vibrate. Add a cardboard roll for the guitar neck.

3. Strum.

110

TIN FOIL MASKS

I always wanted to be a warrior in shining armor. Tin foil is one of the best materials to use for shaping anything from helmets to animals.

THINGS YOU'LL NEED
books on ancient Greece & Rome, tin foil, bowl, scissors

1. Find a picture or illustration of a Greek or Roman soldier's helmet. If you go online, type in "Greek helmet" into your search engine. Pick the simpler looking helmets.

2. Use an upturned bowl (roughly the size of a head) to shape the skullcap part of the helmet. Use one sheet of tin foil to make the cap's lining. Leave the cap lining on the bowl.

3. Use a larger second sheet of tinfoil with a piece that is long enough to come down over the face and cut it so that there is a nose block. You can also create "ear blocks".

4. Lay this shape over the lining you created and tuck the excess tin foil around the edges of the lining to connect both sheets. This will create a double-layered cap. Go forth and fight for the empire.

NOTE! *Wrap foil around a stick to create a metal-looking spear, sword or dagger. By the way, girls like helmets, swords and daggers just as much as the boys. Remember Lady MacBeth?*

ONE-MINUTE MASKS

Now you can be anybody you want.

THINGS YOU'LL NEED
magazine pictures with faces, scissors, 2-sided tape

1. Find a larger photo of a celebrity and cut it out. Cut out the eyes.

2. Place a piece of 2-sided tape on the inside.

3. Tape the photo to your face.

METAL MOLD SHAPES

This is a great way to teach your Kids about molds.

THINGS YOU'LL NEED
molding bowl, tin foil, mixing bowl, flour, water, spoon, dowling, candle

1. Cut 1 sheet of tinfoil that is large enough, so that when you fold it in half, it is still large enough to cover the inside of the molding bowl (any bowl will do).

2. Press the folded tin foil into the bowl. You can always add another layer of tin foil to make the mold thicker and sturdier.

3. Mix the flour and water in the mixing bowl so that it turns into a watery-like clay.

4. Carefully spoon the flour-water mixture into the tin foil mold. You don't have to fill the entire mold.

5. Leave it to dry. When the clay is half dry, insert a round stick the size of a candle (dowling), or a candle itself, right through the center to the bottom.

6. Once the clay is dry, remove the shape, peel off the tin foil, and take out the stick or candle.

7. You can turn the shape over and use it as a dome. Either way, in the hole, you can stick the candle part way down, turning the shape into a candle-holder.

8. If you want to use it in its original bowl shape, you may have to square off the bottom by sanding it to make sure it rests stably on a surface.

OUTDOOR ACTIVITIES

SOUND EXPERIENCES
BLADE GRASS WHISTLE

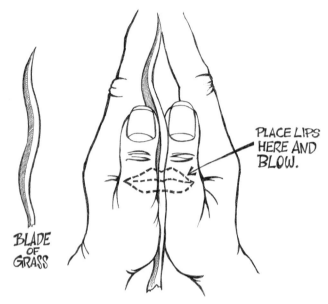

PLACE LIPS HERE AND BLOW.

BLADE OF GRASS

It takes practice. Experiment with different sizes of grass blades.

THINGS YOU'LL NEED
blade of grass

1. Find a long blade of grass that is not too thin.
2. Put the blade between your thumbs. The back of your thumbs should be facing you.
3. Center the blade in the little space below the knuckles.
4. Press your lips to the space and blow.

WHAT YOUR EYES DON'T HEAR

This exercise opens up a new world for people of all ages. We take our eyes for granted and don't realize how much more we can learn and understand about our world through our other senses.

THINGS YOU'LL NEED
blindfold

1. Blindfold the participant.
2. Lock you arms together and walk arm in arm.
3. Ask the blindfolded participant what they hear, smell and feel.
4. Walk a familiar route for about 15 minutes.

AIR EXPERIENCES
SMALL PAPER KITE

Sure, you can buy a kite.

THINGS YOU'LL NEED

1 sheet of 8 1/2 x 11" (21.59 x 27.94 cm) typing paper,
8-inch (20 cm) BBQ shish kabob stick,
masking tape or any type of plastic tape, 1 roll of string 200' (60.96 m),
a bigger stick or a piece of cardboard to wind the kite string on, scissors, ribbon

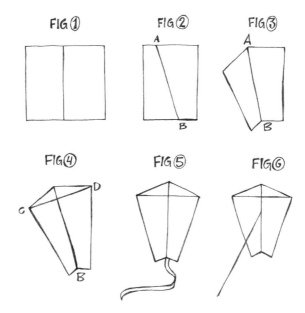

1. Fold a sheet of 8½ x 11" (21.59 x 27.94 cm) paper in half to 8½ x 5½" (21.59 x 13.97 cm).

2. Fold it again along the diagonal line 'A' (figure 2).

3. Fold back one side forming the kite shape (figure 3).

4. Tape down the fold line 'A-B'.

5. Put the BBQ stick down from point 'C' to 'D' and tape it in place (figure 4).

6. Tape a 6-foot piece of ribbon at the point marked 'B', the bottom of the kite (figure 5).

7. Turn the kite over.

8. Get the front flap to stand up straight by folding it back and forth.

9. Punch a hole in the flap at point 'E', about a third of the way down from the top point 'A' (figure 6).

10. Tie one end of the string to the hole and wind the rest onto the cardboard or bigger stick.

SMALL PARACHUTE

Sure, you can buy a parachute.

THINGS YOU'LL NEED
1 garbage bag, packing tape, string, action figure or stuffed animal

1. Cut open the garbage bag so it is one sheet.

2. Cut out the largest hexagon shape you can.

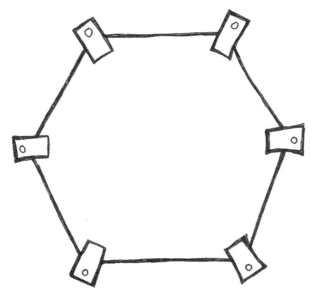

3. Cut 6 square pieces of packing tape and attach them to each point of the hexagon. Fold the tape over on each point, leaving the non-stick part of the tape on the outside. Make sure the clips extend far enough beyond the points so that when you make a hole in the tape, you won't puncture the bag.

4. Make a small hole in each of the clips you created.

5. Tie a 2-foot (.6 m) length of string to each clip.

6. With the parachute lying flat, gather the 6 strings together and pull up so that the points begin to come off the ground.

7. Tape, tie or clip together the strings at the gathering point. You should have some extra string left beyond the gathering point.

8. Using the extra string, attach your choice of an action figure or small, stuffed animal. You can also use a small saltshaker or bottle. The parachutist can be just about anything as long as it has a bit of weight.

9. Gently fold (don't roll) the parachute to as small a size as you can. Wrap the string gently around the folded parachute.

10. Drop the parachute from an elevated deck, or throw the package into the air.

NOTE! *Experiment with different sizes of parachutes.*

WINTER FUN

HOMEMADE SLED

Sure, you can buy a sled. But do you really want to go through life without trying garbage bags?

THINGS YOU'LL NEED
1 large garbage bag, 2 smaller garbage bags

1. Cut 2 openings at the corners of one end of the large garbage bag. Make the openings large enough to get legs through.

2. Put on the garbage bag and secure it as high up on your body as you can.

3. Put the 2 smaller garbage bags on your boots and secure them at the ankles.

4. Run into the down slope and slide into a sitting position. Be aware, it will be a challenge to run with slick garbage bags on your boots. Your plastic layered butt and feet will ensure a quick ride. Spectators will thrown money at you (to buy a sled).

NOTE! The steeper the slope, the more success you'll have. CAUTION! Examine the slope carefully for rocks and serious bumps, otherwise, this could be dangerous.

SNOWBALL BOMBERS

If you keep the snowballs small, this will be a lot of fun. So, keep them SMALL!

THINGS YOU'LL NEED
2 poles, large sheet, snow

1. Set up 2 polls and attach a large sheet, like a volleyball net, only larger. Make sure that people on one side cannot see the heads of the people on the other side.

2. Make your snowballs.

3. Lob the snowballs over the sheet. People acting as targets on the other side cannot move. As a precaution, the targets should cover their faces.

4. Score a point for every hit.

SNOW GOLF

Who says you can't golf in winter? FOUR!

THINGS YOU'LL NEED
frisbee, short irons (the 8, 9, & sand wedge), colored plastic golf balls

1. In a snow-covered park, flat open field, or on a large lawn, throw out a frisbee as a target – not too far away.

2. Hit your balls. The closest to the target wins that round – get it – round, like a frisbee.

SOME THINGS IN LIFE ARE FREE

More and more local, community organizations are offering families many opportunities to enjoy free programs and activities all year round. Places like libraries and museums have become more than just buildings to visit and see things. Now, many of them have developed free programs designed for Parents and Kids.

You can find out a lot by going to their website or by calling and talking to a Community Program Coordinator or a Program Manager. Here's where to look: community leagues, libraries, museums, municipal government, provincial, county or state government, and faith-based organizations.

If you like to surf the net, type this into your search engine: "free community programs" (add the name of your town or city). Many of you will be amazed at what you find.

CHAPTER 3

TRAVELLING TOGETHER

SURVIVING THE TRIP

There are three unavoidable realities about travelling with Kids. The first is, Kids of all ages get bored on the road. Secondly, they will make a mess, whether it's in your car, on the plane, the train or the boat. Last, and definitely not least, they will have to go – and go – and go – always at the worst time.

It took many miles and trips for me to realize that travelling with Kids is not about "getting there". It's truly about the journey. It's an adventure. Interestingly, the origin of the word "adventure" comes from the Latin, "aventura", which means "to arrive". But the Middle English meaning, "a venture", is more like it.

So, if you plan to venture out there with your Kids, remember, you can't wrap them in plastic and drug them to sleep. You will have to assert your role as Captain of the ship and Commander of the voyage.

TIPS TO TRAVEL

1. **Pack less**. The more you take, the more you have to track. Finding everything in a crowded hotel room or cabin can make or break a Dad on the last day of the trip. Think small. Buy those travel size items, like toothpaste, soap and shampoo.

2. **Make a packing list for each person**. For the Kids who can write, enlist them as the chief scribe for their own list. *NOTE! Kids hate long lists, which works out in the end. Even they will want to take less.*

3. **Use containers and zip-type bags for small things**. Crayons, games and small toys will be easier to pack and categorize.

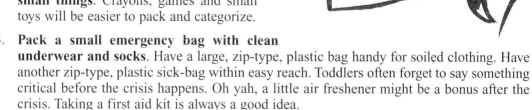

4. **Pack a small emergency bag with clean underwear and socks**. Have a large, zip-type, plastic bag handy for soiled clothing. Have another zip-type, plastic sick-bag within easy reach. Toddlers often forget to say something critical before the crisis happens. Oh yah, a little air freshener might be a bonus after the crisis. Taking a first aid kit is always a good idea.

5. **If you're travelling with small Kids, go to the dollar store and buy a bag full of items including toys and games**. Every 30 minutes or so, pull out a new item. You can keep them engaged for long periods of time this way. Another trick is to dip into their toy boxes and file unused toys for future trips. Everything old is new again.

6. **Stop frequently along the way**. The final destination is not the only exciting part of the trip. Take in the sites along the way: mountains, historic sites, fruit stands, parks, animals, weird stores or buildings, and even a missspellled sign. It gives everyone a chance to stretch their legs and something to talk about between stops. When I'm driving, I like to stop every 2 hours for a break. Travelling with Kids makes me tired. A tired driver falls asleep at the wheel.

7. **Dress and pack for travel weather**. If you live in cold weather climates, the biggest challenge is to dress the Kids for both the weather and the confines of the mode of transportation. Big winter coats take up a lot of space inside most vehicles. Don't wear them inside the car. Instead, dress the Kids in easy to manage layers (T-shirt, long sleeve top, and a lighter coat). Pack the bigger coats in the trunk. Pack slippers or slip-on runners for the hotel. We once spent an entire weekend living in our boots.

8. **Think safety**. Kids can wander away and get lost in a crowd. Keep photos of your Kids in a wallet to show people if you and the Kids get separated. Give a photo of yourself to each of your Kids for the same reason. If you have a mobile phone and know it is operational where you're going, get your Kids to memorize your phone number. You can also write it on the back of all the photos. I've heard of some Parents taking 2-way radios along, assigning the second radio to the most responsible Kid. This is especially helpful at campsites.

9. **Accept the fact that things will get dirty**. Tell yourself that you will not look at the bottom of your vehicle until you get back from the trip. Take along some clothesline-type clips and some line to hang wet clothes wherever you're staying. Deodorant for the shoes and boots will save your nose. A fabric spray for socks can help if you're not always close to a washing machine.

10. **It's not about how far you go**. Many cities and communities have campgrounds nearby. A night under the stars roasting hotdogs at a campfire brings out the Kid in all of us. Travelling to a different community nearby is an adventure. One-day excursions are easy to plan and they don't have to cost a lot. Even if you take lots of pictures, the enduring memories will resonate with your Kids. They will talk about the adventures you helped create – no matter how big or small in scope – for the rest of their lives.

122

GETTING READY

PLANNING

Planning is everything. Getting the Kids involved from the very beginning really helps make for a better trip. Otherwise, the last minute rush guarantees that you'll start the trip with everyone feeling frustrated.

THINGS YOU'LL NEED
snacks, pads & pencils

1. Prepare a plate of easy-to-eat snacks.

2. Set out paper and writing tools for family members who can write.

3. Get everyone around the kitchen or dining table.

4. Explain the trip to them: the destination, how long it will take to get there, and how long you're staying.

5. Let them ask questions. When they get around to the question about what they can take or what they should pack, take charge.

6. Make a list of things you can easily buy where you're going, like diapers and food.

7. Next, figure out underwear and socks. Help them calculate how much they will need. If you know there will be laundry facilities, take enough for half the trip (if longer than a weekend).

8. For clothing, start with what they're going to wear during the ride to the destination.

9. For colder destinations, think in layers.

10. Stick to your guns. They objective is to pack as little as possible. Minimize the number of items that are thick or take up a lot of space. It's easier to pack T-shirts versus fleece tops.

11. Figure out footwear. Plan to use one separate bag or box for all the footwear.

12. Have each person make a list of personal items. Make a list of travel size items you can get, like soaps and toothpaste.

13. Make a list of first aid items, sprays and medicines. Plan to pack these items into one kit.

14. If you're going to a lake, fishing, camping or skiing, use items in more than one way. For example, a sleeping bag can be used as a blanket in the car. A thick fleece top or a beach towel can be rolled up as a pillow for the trip. If each child rolls one thing as a pillow, that's one less thing to pack in their suitcase.

15. Decide on distractions for the drive: games, books, toys and electronics (cameras, DVD player, MP3 players, reading light). Obviously, you'll have additional things on your list based on the nature of the trip, such as sporting equipment.

16. Unless you know that you can buy batteries where you're going, then put extra batteries on your list of things to pack.

17. Make up a snack list. Keep it simple. You'll find a list of snack suggestions in this chapter. Take just enough snacks for the ride there. You can always buy more snacks for the ride back.

PACKING FOR THE VEHICLE

It's an art. I learned the hard way because, for the longest time, I drove a small car. Packing everything really meant cramming everything in.

THINGS YOU'LL NEED
suitcases, garment bag, boxes, zip-type bags of all sizes

1. Put all the nicer clothes (if your trip requires it) in the same garment bag so they can lay flat.

2. Tightly roll socks and underwear. Stuff them into zip-type bags and, if possible, pack them into the shoes or boots. This creates more room in the suitcases for other things. The zip-type bags prevent the smell of the footwear from becoming the smell of the vehicle.

3. Pack all the footwear together in a box or a smaller suitcase.

4. Use soft shell suitcases or bags for clothing. This will give you the opportunity to squeeze some things in between the bags.

5. Put tissue paper in between clothes to prevent wrinkling. If you put tissue paper on your face, it won't do anything for your wrinkles.

6. In zip-type bags, pack sprays, creams, powders, or anything containing liquid. Then, pack them in the middle of the clothes to reduce the possibility of anything breaking.

7. Wrap a robe or sweat suit around everything in your bag. If your bag becomes exposed to a lot of moisture or water, this outside layer of clothing can absorb any water that may get inside. If I'm taking more than one outdoor coat or jacket, I'll first lay one open jacket into the bag, pack some clothes in it, then close the jacket. I'll lay a second jacket over top in the same way and create another layer.

8. Pack the first aid kit and recreational items (such as balls or frisbees) last, so that they're easily accessible when you need to stop for an emergency or take a travel break.

9. Pack an extra empty bag for souvenirs. Stuff it with towels, newspapers or bags, so that it will accurately simulate the amount of space it will take once it is actually filled with souvenirs. Of course, you can throw away the bags and newspapers, but you'll have to accommodate the towels somewhere on the way back.

10. Pack a wet cloth into one zip-type bag, and a dry cloth in another zip-type bag. Have a roll of paper towel handy, too, which you can store under a front seat. When a spill or anything else happens, you're ready to deal with the 'icky' stuff.

11. TAKE A SMALL, PORTABLE, VACUUM APPLIANCE!

124

THE TRAVELLING TREAT BAG

THINGS YOU'LL NEED
in-car bag filled with toys and simple games
This works for hours.

1. Go to a local dollar or value store that carries inexpensive small toys and party games.

2. Load up a bag filled with a variety of items. Twenty dollars will buy you a whack-load.

3. Over time, dispense the items to keep the troops distracted. You can also use them as a reward or a bribe.

PACKING FOR INTERNATIONAL TRAVEL

THINGS YOU'LL NEED
patience, knowledge of current security issues

1. Contact your local airport authority or check the Transport Security Commission website for the most current information.

2. Pack small knives or sharp objects with the baggage that will be checked (not the carry-on baggage).

3. Keep your house keys and car keys with you. If you have pointy, sharp things attached to your key chain, take them off and either leave them at home or pack them in the baggage to be checked.

4. You can carry on most electronics: camcorders, mobile phones, laptop computers, PDAs (personal data assistants) and pagers. Once again, check with the airport authority to be sure you're up to date with the current information.

5. Cross pack items with your Kids. In other words, put some of the basic stuff they need in your bag and put some of your basic stuff in their bags. That way, if a bag goes missing, you will all have something to wear.

6. Bring your own snacks. Even if the airline you're flying on offers a dinner, you may have to wait for a while. The snacks you can buy on the plane will cost you an arm and a leg. Snacks also come in handy during layovers in airports at a time when stores and restaurants are closed and you don't have enough coins to harvest the coin machines.

7. Put clear identification tags on your baggage. You might even consider using a special colored ribbon. It seems that 90 percent of the bags these days are black. I once waited 20 minutes longer than I had to at the baggage carousel because my bag (which passed me a dozen times) looked like all the others.

8. CARRY A PASSPORT!

TRAVELLING DISTRACTIONS
LICENSE PLATE POKER

This game works best on a 4-lane highway. It definitely appeals to the teenagers. It doesn't matter what state, province or country the license plate is from, it still works.

THINGS YOU'LL NEED
pencil, paper

1. Each person claims a license plate of a passing vehicle or a vehicle being passed.

2. The player records the license number and does not share the letters or numbers with anyone else. You'll need a bit of an honor system to play.

3. Then, one license plate is recorded, which everyone can share. In poker, this is the equivalent of the community cards.

4. Each player then picks whatever values from the community license plate, and adds them to their own to make the best hand. For any hand, you can only use 5 values of any combination of letters and numbers.

5. Once the final hands have been determined by each player, they're all "called", which means that everyone has to show their hand. The best hand wins a point. (Of course, any family can make up its own betting process.)

Because there are no suits to work with, the combinations and values work as follows.

1. As in cards, each hand has 5 playable units, which can be letters only, numbers only or a combination of letters and numbers.

2. The letter 'A' is the highest valued letter. The number '1' is the highest number value. The numbers are dealt with as single integers from '1 to 9'. They cannot be combined to make any numbers higher than '9'.

3. Letters are more valuable because there are more letters than numbers and they're harder to match or sequence.

4. Letters and numbers can be sequenced, like a poker straight. Eg. ABCDE, 12345, VWXYZ, 56789

5. Similar numbers and letters can work as pairs, 3-of-a-kind, 4-of-a-kind and – because this is not, in fact, based on a card system – 5-of-a-kind works, too.

Here are the rankings from the highest to lowest. Letters are always higher in value than numbers. 5 letter sequences are higher than 5 number sequences. All sequences (letters or numbers) are higher than 5-of-a-kind (letters or numbers). 5-of-a-kind (letters or numbers) is higher than 4-of-a-kind (letters or numbers). 4-of-a-kind (letters or numbers) is higher than a full house (letters or numbers). A full house (3 of a kind and 2 of a kind, letters or numbers in any combination – number – number, letter – letter, letters and numbers) is higher than 3-of-a-kind (letters or numbers). ***NOTE!** In a full house, 3 letters and 2 numbers is higher than 3 numbers and 2 letters. 3-of-a-kind (letters or numbers) is higher than pairs (letters or numbers).*

SILENCE IS GOLDEN

This actually works. Trust me.

THINGS YOU'LL NEED
the promise of a treat

1. Challenge everyone to a game of silence.

2. The one who remains silent the longest wins a treat from the 'Treat Bag'.

3. At your discretion, give everyone a treat if you feel you've recovered from the noise stress.

VISUAL SCAVENGER HUNT

This is educational. It takes a little prep work, but it's worth it. It gives Kids and Dads a reason to look out the window. The driver should keep his eyes on the road.

THINGS YOU'LL NEED
a list for everyone, pencils

1. Make a list of things that you'll likely see on your trip. Include words and names, which might be seen on signs. Think of 10 to 20 things. Include at least a couple of weird things – like road-kill or 2 people kissing – or something unique, like a statue or landmark, which you know you'll see in a particular town or area you're passing through.

2. Copy the same list for everyone.

3. When someone sees something on the list, they call it out and check it off their list. The others cross it off, too.

4. Once the list is done, add up the check marks. The one with the most check marks wins.

WHAT'S IN THE FIRST AID KIT?

This is educational, and it's an opportunity to share all those war stories.

THINGS YOU'LL NEED
a first aid kit

1. Delegate the responsibility of managing the kit to one of the Kids.

2. Take one item out at a time.

3. Ask everyone to guess what it is.

4. Then, if it has a label, ask the kit manager to read the label. If no one knows, tell them what it is. (This means you have to bone up on the kit contents.)

5. Ask your Kids what the item should be used for.

6. If there is more to explain about the item, take the time to educate them.

7. Award treats at your discretion.

NOTE! See FIRST AID KITS on page 152.

TRAVELLING SNACK ATTACKS

I hate crumbs, gums, and anything that melts. My car eats more food than the Kids. The key to success here is stocking up on snacks that do not leave a huge mess behind. Be sure you have a dedicated garbage bag and a small, portable, battery-operated or car-powered vacuum cleaner.

CONTAINERS FOR FOOD & BEVERAGES

THINGS YOU'LL NEED
**small plastic containers with lids, zip-type bags,
small cooler with plastic freeze packs, water bottles**

1. Use the smaller plastic containers with lids for things like cut veggies, fruits and cheeses. (I find that things like veggies and fruits in zip-type bags are harder for Kids to manipulate with their hands.)

2. Use the zip-type bags for chips, pretzels and nuts.

3. If you're anal, put the fruits and veggies into the zip-type bags and then into the plastic containers.

4. Use water bottles for beverages, even if you have cans of pop or juice. Cans are a disaster waiting to happen.

5. A small cooler with freeze packs will keep veggies, fruits and beverages cool and fresh.

SNACKS

THINGS YOU'LL NEED
bite-sized food, easy-to-handle beverages

1. If you're cheap, you'll prepare your own snacks. But if you buy stuff, get small bags of everything, which you can keep in a larger container or bag.

2. For veggies and fruits, choose those that create the least mess: celery, carrots, tomatoes, grapes, and apples.

3. For dry snacks, same thing: choose those that create less of a mess. The trick here is to either buy off-the-shelf snacks in small bags or prepare your own snacks and put them in small zip-type bags. Chips, pretzels, and nuts will still create a mess, but, at least, they're manageable.

4. For cheese snacks, I recommend those cheese sticks. They're packaged well and tend to be consumed quickly. You can slice your own cheese, or take wrapped cheese slices, but you'll want to keep these cool.

5. Granola bars are an alternative to trail mixes. You can take this one step further and pre-slice the bars into bite-sized chunks, which you would put into a container or zip-type bag.

6. Juice-box containers are the easiest and best way to control the flow of drinking. Alternatively, you can transfer canned or boxed pop and juices to water bottles that have control tops.

7. Stay away from taking snacks, which don't hold up well, like bananas and milk. If they're dropped or spilled, they'll eventually transform the car's atmosphere into something distasteful.

8. Avoid snacks that crumble too easily and stain everything – like cheesies.

CHAPTER 4

PARTYING TOGETHER
SURVIVING THE CELEBRATION

The party thing drives me nuts. They're labor intensive, often rushed, and usually turn into mayhem. By the party's end, Parents are weary, Kids are on a sugar high, and you're left wondering if the cost was worth it. Moms traditionally plan parties like weddings. Dads are delegated as assistant taskmasters.

The evolution of organized party centers is a response to the need time-challenged Parents have for convenience. Let's face it, the biggest issue is the clean up. As a result, more parties occur outside the home and at pools, gymnasiums, and franchise party outlets.

I'm not saying this is a bad thing; it doesn't change the fact that Dads, regardless of circumstances, are challenged when it comes to having a party that doesn't involve high balls and cue sticks.

PARTY TIPS

1. **Accept your limitations**. Keep the party small. It's a simple strategy. Less people do more things. More people do fewer things. From my experience, my Kids routinely play with less than a handful of children. Just put the question to them. "If you could invite up to 5 of your best friends to a party, who would you ask?" Pick a number that guarantees an even split if you're planning games with 2 teams. Don't forget to count siblings. The Kid who has a dozen or more best friends will be President or Prime Minister one day. If the life-long plan for your Kid is political success, go ahead and knock yourself out. Remind your Kids that they can invite different friends to different parties during the year. The idea here is to teach them to choose people who fit the event.

2. **Choose a location that suits the nature of the party**. Don't be afraid to have a party at home.

3. **Involve your Kids in everything from the very beginning**. The theme and activities will be meaningless if they have no say.

4. **Plan everything well in advance**. Every family is busy. If you're a single Dad, planning an event can be particularly challenging owing to the number of schedules in play between 2 households.

5. **Think small**. Make everything small: bite-sized food and snacks, small PAPER plates and PLASTIC cups. Kids like to munch endlessly. Why fight it? Keep the food in one place where they can quickly grab what they want (preferably with tongs or toothpicks). You can also divide up the number of bite-sized consumables according to the number of participants. Assign a plate for each one, identified by a nametag or card. If you're partying at home and your room space permits, keep the food and beverages in the kitchen.

6. **Limit the length of the party**. Kids wear out quickly in groups. Plan on 1 to 2 hours for toddlers; no more than 3 hours for the older Kids. Major parties for your older teenagers are much like adult parties. Good luck with those adventures.

7. **Post a "WASH YOUR HANDS" sign in the bathroom**. Use a liquid soap dispenser instead of a bar of soap. Use paper towels that can be disposed of easily. Accept the fact that your bathroom will be a designated zone of mass destruction. Periodically, check the status of your bathroom and do frequent mini cleanups using disinfecting towelettes. Don't forget to wipe down the liquid soap dispenser.

8. **Include yourself in at least one game or activity**. Kids love to see their Dads play.

9. **Plan at least one activity that will settle the Kids down towards the end of the party**. You could recite poetry or drug their pop cans, but a video would probably work better.

10. **Think safety**. Be aware of any health issues, allergies, or skill limitations (can a Kid swim?) relating to invited guests. When you're going to an outside location, plan the security details in advance.

133

BIRTHDAY PARTY

134

PLANNING THE B'DAY PARTY

There are as many concepts and themes as there are Kids on the planet. Themes change as fast as Kids' interests change. It's an event for an individual, as opposed to a Halloween party, which offers more common themes for any number of people. You'll find that the favorite activity usually leads the way in planning the party.

THEMES

THINGS YOU'LL NEED
time to research & discuss

1. Go to your Kid's room and note down all the things you see that tell you what they're in to.

2. Make mental notes of the TV programs, movies and music they like.

3. Do the same around their physical interests: sports, physical activities.

4. Think about the hobbies or special activities they enjoy.

5. Present this list and ask your Kid to pick either the top thing in each category or the top 3 things. This becomes the short list.

6. Ask for a list of friends they would like to invite.

7. If you don't already know their friends well, ask your Kid about them and what they like to do. The objective is to determine a common interest in activities.

8. Set a date.

9. Get contact information for the guests.

10. Divvy up the responsibilities. Get everyone in the family involved.

135

B'DAY INVITATIONS

THINGS YOU'LL NEED
cards or computer paper

1. You can either buy cards or, if you want to simplify the process, use your computer and printer to create simple invitations.

2. My biggest beef is not having enough information when I receive an invitation.

   a. Include the following: the date, time, location and a map, especially if you live in a hard-to-find location.

   b. Tell Parents when the Kids should be dropped off and picked up. Advise Parents if their attendance is optional.

   c. If you're feeding the Kids, tell Parents when you'll feed them and basically what you'll feed them. This helps them manage their own dinner plans on that day.

   d. Ask for information about allergies and any physical limitations.

   e. Include a phone number and email and ask a response to the invitation by a certain date.

   f. Briefly explain the theme. This will give Parents an idea of what kind of gift to bring. Or, if you're that type, let them know a gift is not necessary. Don't tell them a gift is optional because it can make Parents feel awkward.

   g. Recommend a dress code. The last thing you need is someone showing up dressed to the 9's when the party plans include mud wrestling.

3. If you know your Kid is responsible, you can ask them to hand out the invitations. My recommendation is that you mail them, or email an invitation if you're able to get email addresses.

4. Get the invitations out at least 3 weeks in advance. Most families have plans, especially with Kids who are involved with sports and other activities.

136

SAMPLE B'DAY INVITATION

You're invited to Birthday Girl's 8th birthday party.
Date & time: day, date, 1:30 pm to 4:30 pm

Location: 123 our street
(Please see the map for directions.)

Theme: Little Diva
Dress: play-casual with running shoes
We will be playing a soccer game.

Party snacks: during party
Meal: hot dogs, cake & ice cream starting at 3:00

If your child has any allergies or physical limitations,
please let us know in advance.

Please bring your child between 1:00 and 1:30.
Please pick up your child between 4:00 and 4:30.
Parents' attendance is optional.
Let us know if you plan to accompany your child.

Please respond to this invitation by the day & date.
Phone or email. 555-5555 parent@emailaddress.com
Small gifts are welcome.

B'DAY TREAT BAGS

THINGS YOU'LL NEED
zip-type bags, treats (store-bought)

1. Local dollar-type or craft stores offer a selection of treats ranging from small toys to candies.

2. If you want to avoid allergy issues, stick to small toys.

3. Avoid things like stick-on tattoos, putty, or things that spray out of cans. Some Parents may not appreciate them. The Dads who have to clean up certainly won't.

4. Keep the treats generic if you have Kids of both sexes attending.

5. You might want to ask your Kid to help out with the process. Of course, if it were completely up to them, you'd go broke filling the treat bags.

6. It's not about quantity. You can find some inexpensive items like plastic or fold-up cloth frisbees, playing cards or trading cards, small plastic toys, juggling balls, plastic bracelets and rings, finger puppets, whistles, balloons, and small stuffed animals or small action figures. Always check the clearance area of a toy store. You might luck out.

7. If the Kids attending the party are very young, avoid treats that can cause choking.

138

B'DAY PARTY RECIPES

You can always buy the pre-made stuff. Nowadays, baking departments in major grocery stores create pretty incredible stuff and decorate it to your specifications. If you only bake a cake or cupcakes once in your life, use these 2 simple recipes. Yes, they involve lots of sugar. C'mon, it's their birthday.

EASIEST B'DAY CAKE EVER

POUND CAKE STUFF
3 cups cake flour, 1/2 tsp. baking soda, 1 tsp. baking powder,
1 lb. (500 g) sugar, 1/2 tsp. salt, 1 lb. (500 g) butter, 6 large eggs,
1/2 cup buttermilk, 2 tsp. pure vanilla extract, icing, whipped cream

THINGS YOU'LL NEED
sifter, stirring spoon, large mixing bowl, mixer, tube cake pan,
toothpicks, candles

1. Sift the flour, baking soda and baking powder in the mixing bowl.

2. Stir in the sugar and salt.

3. Melt the butter in the microwave at medium power and drop it into the bowl.

4. Crack the eggs into the bowl.

5. Use your mixer on a lower speed and start blending the stuff.

6. Pour the buttermilk into the bowl.

7. Drop in the vanilla extract.

8. Rev up the mixer to a medium speed for 2 minutes and then on high for another 3 minutes.

9. If the mixture is too thick, add a little more buttermilk.

10. Look out for the lumps. Break up the lumps if you have any.

12. Preheat the oven to 325°F (160°C).

13. Grease the tube cake pan with butter.

14. Lightly flour the buttered pan. Shake off the excess flour from the pan.

15. Pour the mix into the pan.

16. Bake the cake for about 1 hour and 20 minutes.

17. Do the toothpick test. Stick a wooden toothpick into the thickest part of the cake. It should be dry when you pull it out, which means that the cake is done.

18. Let the cake cool for 20 minutes

19. Cover it with either store-bought icing or whipped cream.

20. Stick candles into it. Like, you're a hero, man.

139

EASIEST B'DAY CUP CAKES EVER

CUP CAKE STUFF

3 cups cake flour, 1 tsp. baking powder, 1/2 tsp. baking soda, 1 tsp. salt,
4 large eggs, 2 tsp. vanilla extract, 1 1/3 cups sugar,
1 1/2 sticks unsalted butter, 1 1/2 cups buttermilk

THINGS YOU'LL NEED

cupcake tin, cupcake liners, 2 mixing bowls, stirring spoon,
mixer, whisk, toothpicks

1. Line the cupcake tin with liners. Share a couple of one-liners.

2. In a small bowl, mix together the flour, baking powder, soda, and salt.

3. In a large bowl, mix together the eggs and the vanilla extract.

4. Drop the sugar into the large bowl with the eggs and mix it slowly with a mixer.

5. Melt the butter in the microwave at medium power and then mix it with the eggs, followed by the buttermilk.

6. Add a third of the dry ingredients (the stuff still in the small bowl) into the larger bowl, mixing everything gently together using a whisk.

7. Repeat this process twice with the remaining dry ingredients.

8. Stir the batter gently with a stirring spoon until most of the lumps disappear. You can also use the mixer on a slower speed.

9. Once the batter is ready, fill the cupcake liners about ⅔ full.

10. Heat the oven up to 325°F (160°C).

11. Bake the cupcakes for about 20 minutes, or until a toothpick test comes out clean.

12. Cool the cupcakes for 5 minutes. Then take them out and put them on a cooling rack for about an hour before adding the frosting or icing. The paper liners should remain attached to the cupcakes. Don't eat the paper liners.

140

B'DAY PARTY ACTIVITIES

If you're stuck for activities, here is a theme that works for Kids of all ages, from young Kids to Teenagers. It will work very well if you have other Parents involved.

B'DAY OLYMPICS

THINGS YOU'LL NEED
activity stations, props, stopwatches, judge's pad & pencil, prizes

1. Design a few stations, each with its own activity.

2. Break the participants up into smaller groups of 4 to 6 people.

3. Assign a separate Parent-judge for each station. You may have to use the same judge at more than 1 station. This will determine how quickly you get through the entire course of activities.

4. Each judge will explain the activity to the group that arrives at their station.

5. Once all the groups have gone through all the stations, the judges get together to determine the winners. Score by team only. First place gets 5 points, second place, 3 points, and third place, 1 point. Total up the points.

6. Award prizes to each team.

141

OLYMPIC ACTIVITIES

1. **CRACKER WHISTLING**. You'll need a box of basic soup crackers. Set up a plastic or paper sheet on the ground. Set a chair on it. Each participant sits in the chair. They have 30 seconds to chew 2 crackers at the same time and, without swallowing, try to whistle. Not as easy as you think. For each participant who is able to whistle, record a check mark for that team.

2. **EGG ROLLING RACE**. Set up a short racing lane. Give each participant a hard boiled egg and a chopstick. One at a time, each participant races against the clock. They have 30 seconds to push the egg to the finish line using only the chopstick. If the distance is shorter, reduce the race time. Record a check mark for each participant who crosses the finish line.

3. **FEATHER RACE**. Set up a short racing lane that ends with a table and a bowl. Give each participant a spoon and a light fluffy feather. Have them place the feather on the spoon. They have 30 seconds to get the feather into the bowl. They cannot touch the feather with anything but the spoon. Record a check mark for each participant who crosses the finish line.

4. **TISSUE RACE**. Set up as long a racing lane as you can. Cut a small circle of tissue paper, about 2 inches (5 cm) in diameter. Give each participant a tin foil plate. The object is for the team to work together and fan the circular piece of tissue to the finish line. Time each team.

5. **BLAH CHARADES**. In each group, one participant is chosen, and given a word they have to communicate through physical actions. They can also speak, but only with phrases or expressions using the word, "blah". Each member of the team has to act out a different word that is chosen each time by the judge. The words should be simple and related to the party theme. Record a check mark for each word correctly guessed by the team.

6. **SCORING**. Score by team only. Total up the check marks or the fastest times of each team according to each activity. For each activity, first place gets 5 points, second place, 3 points, and third place, 1 point. Total up the points.

DAD WILL YOU PLEASE TELL GEOFF WE'RE NOT DOPE CHECKING ANYONE, JUST CAUSE HE LOST THE EGG ROLL!

HALLOWEEN PARTY

143

PLANNING THE HALLOWEEN PARTY

Halloween takes care of itself. No matter how old your Kids are, everyone can participate and have fun. It's up to you how far you go and much you have in the way of resources. The key is to come up with a theme that most people can easily work with. If you want your guests to participate in activities, then a simpler costume works better. Masks and complicated costumes make it more difficult to play games. The other reality is that Kids heat up fast in bulky costumes. On Halloween, I wear my pointy alien ears and a T-shirt with all kinds of small, gimmicky things attached to it. I can wear that costume for a long period of time and still perform all kinds of activities. And you should see the looks I get when I'm grocery shopping. "Live long and prosper." Or is it, "Live long and perspire?"

THEMES

THINGS YOU'LL NEED
time to research and discuss

1. Halloween is all the theme you need, but, you can explore sub-themes, too: horror, fantasy, science fiction, sports, music, history, circus – you name it – they're all doorways to ideas. I knew someone who showed up as a TV set once. Go figure.

2. Ask for a list of friends they would like to invite.

3. Set a party date that occurs before Halloween.

4. Get contact information for the guests.

5. Divvy up the responsibilities. Get everyone in the family involved.

HALLOWEEN INVITATIONS

THINGS YOU'LL NEED
cards or computer paper

NOTE! See B'DAY INVITATIONS on page 136.

SAMPLE INVITATION

You're invited to a Halloween Spooktacular Party.
Date & time: day, date, 4:30 pm to 7:30 pm
Location: 123 our street (please see the map for directions)
Theme: anything halloween goes
Dress: simple costume
We will be playing halloween games.

Party snacks: during party
Meal: hot dogs & jello starting at 6:00.

If your child has any allergies or physical limitations,
please let us know in advance.

Please bring your child between 4:00 and 4:30.
Please pick up your child between 7:00 and 7:30.
Parents' attendance & costume are optional.
Let us know if you plan to accompany your child.

Please respond to this invitation by day & date.
Phone or email. 555-5555 parent@emailaddress.com

You need not bring anything other than a desire to have fun.

TREAT BAGS

THINGS YOU'LL NEED
zip-type bags, treats (store-bought)
NOTE! See B'DAY TREAT BAGS on page 138.

1. At Halloween, just about every store from convenience and grocery stores to craft and department stores carry a universe of Halloween items.

2. Rubber insects and squiggly items appeal to both sexes (most of the time).

3. If the Kids attending the party are very young, avoid treats that can cause choking.

145

HALLOWEEN PARTY RECIPES

EYEBALLOWS

STUFF
marshmallows, raisins

THINGS YOU'LL NEED
sharp knife, cutting board, small spoon

1. Take each marshmallow and, on the cutting board, carve out a hollow on one of the flat sides.
2. Spoon out a little peanut butter into the hollow.
3. Squeeze a few raisins into the peanut butter in the hollow so they stay in position.

BONE STICKS

STUFF
ready-to-make breadstick baking dough (store-bought)

THINGS YOU'LL NEED
knife or spoon, baking sheet, parchment paper

1. Instead of making the normal breadsticks, reshape them into a typical bone shape.
2. Cover the baking sheet with parchment paper.
3. Lay out the dough on the parchment paper and using a knife or spoon, shape them into bones.
4. Bake them according to the package instructions.

146

CURSE OF THE MUMMY WIENER

(also known as a HALLOWEENIE)

STUFF
ready-to-make croissant baking dough (store-bought), hot dogs

THINGS YOU'LL NEED
baking sheet, parchment paper

1. Wrap the dogs in dough like a mummy and lay them on parchment paper on the baking sheet.
2. Bake them in the oven at 375°F (190°C) for about 15 minutes.

OH MY GUTS

STUFF
3 cups chow mein noodles,
6 oz. (170 g) package butterscotch or chocolate chips

THINGS YOU'LL NEED
saucepan, stirring spoon, wax paper

1. In a saucepan, melt the chips over low heat, stirring constantly.
2. Remove the melted chips from the heat and stir in the chow mein noodles.
3. Spoon out the guts (as much as 3 doz.) onto the wax paper. Shape doesn't matter.

BUG EYE PUDDING

STUFF
gelatin mix (strawberry or lime) (store-bought), blueberries

THINGS YOU'LL NEED
saucepan, stirring spoon, serving bowls

1. Follow the gelatin package recipe for making it.
2. Pour it out into serving bowls.
3. Add the blueberries – just a few in each bowl. Let it cool.

HALLOWEEN PARTY ACTIVITIES

Unlike the Birthday Olympics, these activities are designed for individual participants. The game is a sensory experience and it is more about how things feel.

HALLOWEEN HORROR OLYMPICS

THINGS YOU'LL NEED
activity stations, blindfolds, paper towels, garbage bags, prizes

1. Design a few stations, each with its own activity.

2. Hand out blindfolds to every participant and have them wait in a different room.

3. On each person's turn, have them put on a blindfold, and then lead them into the horror room.

4. The rules are that they can only use their hands to figure out what they're touching.

5. After they make their guesses, they can remove their blindfold and stay in the room to watch the other participants.

OLYMPIC ACTIVITIES

1. **SNAKES & WORMS**. Cook a bowl full of strand noodles: spaghetti, angel hair, and vermicelli. Fill a plastic box with the noodles. Add some dishwashing liquid to give it a slimy feel. Participants must put their hands in the bowl and guess what it is.

2. **DEAD ANIMAL**. Fill a small balloon with water (not too full) and tie it off. Wrap a feather duster around it and place it in a shoebox. Participants must put their hands in the box and guess what it is. To add some drama to the event, have someone stand nearby with a stick. When the person touches the furry thing, poke the furry animal to make it move.

3. **EYEBALLS**. Fill a bowl with pearl onions and dishwashing liquid. Participants must put their hands in the bowl and guess what it is.

4. **TOADS**. Fill a bowl with small baby pickles. Take some strands cut from elastic bands and push one end of the strand into one end of the pickle. Add a couple of toothpicks (little bones). Participants must put their hands in the bowl and guess what it is.

5. **FINGERS**. Fill a shoebox with carrots. Take some strands cut from elastic bands and push one end of the strand into one end of the carrot. Participants must put their hands in the box and guess what it is.

6. **FISH EGGS**. Fill a bowl with tapioca pudding and dishwashing liquid. Participants must put their hands in the bowl and guess what it is.

7. **SCORING**. The participant with the most correct guesses wins. You can, if you wish, have rewards for the top 3 guessers or – better yet – give everyone a slimy prize.

CHAPTER 5

FIRST AID

SAVING THE SURVIVORS

Besides foreign objects showing up in the worst places on (or in) your Kid, most incidents requiring first aid don't have to become a crisis.

Usually, I ask the question, "Are you going to live?" Between the heaving sobs, they manage to indicate that they'll live another day, if only to make sure that my life with them remains as challenging as possible.

I mean, how many things can go wrong? Bites, burns, sprains, minor cuts, bruises – for most Kids, these things can be handled quite readily with a band-aid. I even give my toddler a band-aid for nausea. It's amazing how they respond positively to a band-aid. A band-aid on a forehead is like a placebo for a headache.

Not everything can be handled with a band-aid, so it's very important to be prepared. Safety organizations, like St. John Ambulance and the Red Cross (American and Canadian), have developed an array of first aid and safety products for use in the home and office. If you're really keen, you can take some safety training. You never know when you're going to have to use the Heimlich Manoeuvre to expel a chicken bone from your Kid's esophagus – or possibly a guest's.

In the meantime, here are some tips you can refer to the moment you hear, "OW!!"

TIPS TO FIRST AID

1. **Have a first aid kit in the house**. That's a no-brainer. Take it with you on trips. One item people don't often include in the kit is a magnifying glass or a strong pair or reading glasses. These are really handy when you have to find and remove a tiny splinter.

2. **Don't panic**. Your Kids need to know that you know what to do (even if you don't) and that everything is going to be okay. If you come down on them or look concerned, they feel even worse. Master the look and behavior of your favorite TV doctor.

3. **Enlist the assistance of other siblings**. This teaches them how to be proactive and responsible during a crisis.

4. **Encourage your Kids to handle minor things like small cuts on their own**. You can still supervise, but the idea is to help them become comfortable with the idea that, in some cases, they can take care of themselves.

5. **If you really don't know what you're doing, have a few contacts you can connect with quickly**. There is no shame in seeking help from people you trust. Bottom line, if you think it's very serious, call 911 or your local emergency number. Make sure everyone knows the local emergency numbers and keep them posted somewhere. Oh yah, and make sure your house address number is very visible from the street.

6. **Sterilize things like tweezers and scissors**. Have rubbing alcohol handy.

7. **Take the time to understand what is happening**. If one of your Kids is frequently experiencing small accidents, it may be their way of getting your attention. So, pay attention. Carelessness needs to be addressed.

8. **Find out about helpful organizations and resources**. For example, St. John Ambulance offers comprehensive, affordable, first aid training programs for Parents and Kids. The Red Cross (American and Canadian) also offers several resources.

9. **Have a basic first aid guide somewhere close**.

10. **A kiss makes everything (minor) better**.

FIRST AID KITS

THINGS YOU'LL NEED

1. **BANDAGES, DRESSINGS AND SWABS**:
   elastic bandages in all sizes
   a roll of 3-inch (7.6 cm) wide gauze
   individually packaged 4-inch (10 cm) sterile gauze pads
   a roll of 1-inch (2.5 cm) bandage tape
   butterfly bandage tape
   sterile dressings or towels
   cotton swabs

2. **MEDICINES, CREAMS, LIQUIDS AND SYRUPS**:
   pain reliever (acetaminophen or ibuprofen)
   anti-inflammatory medicine (ibuprofen)
   antihistamine (diphenhydramine is used for allergic reactions)
   hydrogen peroxide
   skin creams like hydrocortisone cream, calamine lotion and antibiotic creams
   rehydration fluids (such as Pedialyte or Infalyte)

3. **TOOLS**:
   scissors
   tweezers
   flashlight
   eyepatch
   arm sling
   tongue depressors (to be used as a finger splint)
   ice pack
   magnifying glass or reading glasses

NOTE! *The American Academy of Pediatrics now recommends that :"syrup of ipecac" should no longer be used routinely as a poison treatment in the home, and that Dads should safely dispose of the syrup if they still have it.*

 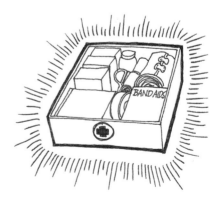

COMMON EMERGENCIES

There is nothing better than training. You and your Kids should take first aid training – period. Also, I am not a doctor, so any advice I am sharing is common knowledge. You should always consult a real doctor, because they spent thousands of dollars in tuition and languished for years in medical school and training.

THE A-B-C's OF C-P-R

THINGS YOU'LL NEED
training

1. 'A' is for "Airway", which consists of positioning a child, opening his airway and making sure it isn't blocked.

2. 'B' is for "Breathing", and is made up of the rescue breaths – breathing into a child's mouth (airway), which you do to a child who has stopped breathing.

3. 'C' is for "Circulation", and can also be thought of as "chest compressions", which is the way that you restore a child's blood flow when their heart has stopped.

4. Rather than feature CPR procedures in detail in this book, I encourage you to take proper training.

NOSE BLEEDS

THINGS YOU'LL NEED
tissues

1. Tell your Kid to lean forward while sitting or standing.

2. Firmly put pressure on the nose by squeezing the lower half of it.

3. Keep the firm pressure going for ten full minutes.

4. After 10 minutes, not before, release your hold to see if it is still bleeding.

4. If the bleeding hasn't stopped, apply pressure for another ten minutes.

5. Call your doctor if the bleeding doesn't stop.

NOTE! *During the 10 minutes, don't check the nose early.*

SUNBURN

THINGS YOU'LL NEED

product containing acetaminophen or ibuprofen, moisturizer, hydrocortisone cream

1. Apply the acetaminophen or ibuprofen for a few days.

2. Use moisturizers and the hydrocortisone cream three times a day, cool baths or wet compresses.

3. Get them to drink lots of fluids.

4. If peeling occurs, continue to apply a moisturizer until the skin heals.

INSECT BITE

THINGS YOU'LL NEED

dull blade, credit card, antibiotic cream

1. Unless your child has an allergy, most bites and stings will cause minor redness, swelling and itching. If you can see the stinger in your Kid's skin, use a dull blade or credit card to scrape it out. Pinching it out can inject more venom into the wound.

2. Once you have it out, apply an antibiotic cream.

MINOR ANIMAL BITES

THINGS YOU'LL NEED

soap, water, antibiotic cream

1. If the bite simply scratches the skin surface, wash the area with soap and water .

2. Apply an antibiotic cream. (I'd be safe and still see a doctor anyway.)

MINOR BLEEDING

THINGS YOU'LL NEED
soap, water, antibiotic cream, sterile dressing

1. If it's a small wound and the bleeding stops quickly, wash the wound with warm, soapy water.

2. Cover it with an antibiotic cream or ointment and apply a sterile dressing.

3. Wash the wound daily and reapply the antibiotic cream and dressing until it's completely healed.

4. If the wound shows signs of infection, becoming red, tender or draining pus, call your doctor.

FINGER INJURY

THINGS YOU'LL NEED
soap, water, sterile dressing

1. When a finger gets caught in a door, wash the fingertip with warm soapy water.

2. Cover it with a sterile dressing to stop any bleeding.

2. If it looks really bad, see your doctor. Then tell the door off.

BURNS

FIRST DEGREE. This is limited to the outer layer of the skin, causing it to be dry, red and painful, but without blistering. A mild or moderate sunburn is an example of a first-degree burn.

SECOND DEGREE. This involves blistering of the skin, and the affected skin will likely appear to be moist.

THIRD DEGREE. All of the skin layers are penetrated and the burned area will be white, charred, firm and leathery. A third degree burn also destroys nerve endings, so your child may not feel pain in the burned area.

THINGS YOU'LL NEED
soap, water, sterile dressing

1. If possible, remove burned clothing or cut it away.

2. For minor burns, soak it in cold water for about fifteen minutes by placing it under running tap water or by covering the area with a cold, wet towel.

3. Place a sterile dressing over the burned area and call your doctor for further instructions, especially for second or third-degree burns, which should almost always be seen by a health professional.

NOTE! *DON'T use ice, butter, or any ointments on the burn and do not break any blisters that have formed.*

CHOKING

THINGS YOU'LL NEED
training in the Heimlich Manoeuvre, emergency numbers

1. If your Kid is choking, but is able to talk or cough, then he is likely to recover on his own.

2. If he is unable to cough or talk or if he is turning blue, you need to do something right away.

3. Call local emergency services.

4. With older Kids you can perform the Heimlich Manoeuvre. Rather than feature the Heimlich Manoeuvre in this book, I recommend that you take first aid training.

NOTE! The Heimlich Manoeuvre cannot be performed on infants under one year of age. They require a different intervention.

TOOTH INJURY

THINGS YOU'LL NEED
glass of milk, gauze

1. If your Kid's tooth is knocked out, place it in a glass of milk.

2. Put gauze over the area that was injured.

3. Take your Kid to a dentist or emergency room as soon as possible after the injury. If attended to quickly, the tooth may be saved.

HEAD INJURY

THINGS YOU'LL NEED
emergency numbers

1. Seek immediate medical attention for further treatment if your Kid has head trauma and loses consciousness, has a seizure, becomes lethargic or drowsy, has frequent vomiting, double vision, or any other changes in his usual personality.

2. For minor head injuries, you should observe your child carefully for at least four to six hours. If problems persist, see your doctor or go to the nearest hospital or clinic.

HIVES

THINGS YOU'LL NEED
antihistamine

1. Use an over-the-counter antihistamine. The large red areas associated with hives usually come and go over 4 to 6 hours. They can disappear from one area and reappear in another.

CHAPTER 6

STAINS, SPOTS, SPILLS & LAUNDRY
SURVIVING THE MESS

It's inevitable. Kids spill things. Dirty hands leave fingerprints everywhere. The laundry piles up in the basket. I used to ignore these things. When my wife decided to ignore it, too, I started to notice things, like smells, stains, and crumbs on the floor. Having come from a world that was oblivious to hygiene at the best of times, I fell into that manly, casual habit of assuming that the mess was not that big a deal and that, somehow, the mess would take care of itself.

Even as a bachelor, laundry was a simple affair and not a science. Throw everything in, add soap and crank the dial. Now there's a soap and additive for every kind and color of clothing. So, I figured that I better write this chapter. My wife insisted. Besides, I would rather spend the time writing than cleaning the bathroom.

TIPS TO A CLEANER WORLD

1. **Educate your Kids and yourself about hygiene**. Thanks to the collective paranoia about all the "icks" (epidemics, pandemics), it's a good idea to learn what we can. Washing hands is a healthy thing to do before and after dinner, and especially after bathroom events. It's even better when they wipe their hands on a towel instead of their clothes.

2. **Stock up on sanitary wipes**. They come in well-designed containers that make it easy for anyone to grab a sheet. Wipe hands and surfaces with them. Get a squeegee for the shower.

3. **Put a lid on it**. I drew a picture for My Kids that shows them how far droplets travel during a flushing cycle. It scared the crap out of them. The lid is no longer left up – as often.

4. **Encourage your Kids to report spills and messes**. Dads are great educators and can turn these upsets into learning experiences. Make them know it's okay to tell you.

5. **Teach your Kids about cleaning products and supplies**. Even a toddler can work an absorbent paper towel.

6. **Stock up on separate supplies for the bathroom, kitchen and the laundry area**. Keep them in those rooms. Distribute paper towels and sanitary wipes strategically around the house.

7. **Break up the cleaning schedule**. Do the bathrooms, kitchen and laundry on different days. Doing a little at a time is much less stressful.

8. **Put a hamper in each Kid's rooms**. Train them to put their laundry IN the hamper. Check the hampers regularly, especially where the younger Kids are concerned.

9. **Bite the dust**. Unhealthy dust accumulates all the time. More Kids and Dads are developing allergies. I have several little duster thingy's. Even my Kids get into the dusting.

10. **Talk trash to your Kids**. I got myself those metal garbage bag holders for the garage and a wastebasket for each of the Kids' rooms and their play area.

WEAPONS OF MESS DESTRUCTION

If you're using store-bought products, read the labels carefully. When using solvents, make sure you keep the area you're working in well ventilated. In general, it is better to blot than rub. Don't use metal spoons or metal containers with bleaches. If you want to avoid getting a ring around a stain, lightly feather out the solution or solvent you're using at the edges. For a larger stain, test a small area first to make sure your solution works. Some stains will require the services of a professional. If you don't know what you're doing, don't experiment.

NOTE! *For pre-treating stains before doing a wash, see the LAUNDRY section on page 162.*

CHEMICAL SUPPLIES

1. **ALCOHOL-BASED SOLUTION.** Buy it at your local grocery or drugstore. Make sure there's no added color or fragrance.
2. **AMMONIA SOLUTION.** Mix 1 tbsp. of ammonia and a ½ cup water.
3. **AMMONIA – MILD DETERGENT SOLUTION.** Mix a few drops of ammonia with a MILD DETERGENT SOLUTION (see #13). Make sure the ammonia doesn't contain coloring or a fragrance.
4. **AMYL ACETATE SOLVENT (BANANA OIL).** Get it in drug stores. Don't use oil-type nail polish remover.
5. **CHLORINE BLEACH SOLUTION.** Mix 1 tsp. of bleach with 1 tbsp. of water. **NOTE!** *Do not use chlorine solution on wool, silk, or spandex.*
6. **DRY CLEANING SOLVENT.** Get it in drug stores, grocery stores, and hardware stores.
7. **DRY SPOTTER.** Mix 1 part mineral oil and 8 parts DRY CLEANING SOLVENT.
8. **ENZYME DETERGENT SOLUTION.** Mix a ½ tsp. of liquid detergent containing enzyme and ½ cup warm water.
9. **HYDROGEN PEROXIDE.** Use a 3% solution sold as a mild antiseptic in drug stores. Don't use the stronger solution sold in cosmetic departments for bleaching hair.
10. **LARD.** This can be found in your local grocery store.
11. **LAUNDRY PRE-TREATMENT SPRAYS.** These are available in grocery stores.
12. **MILD DETERGENT SOLUTION.** Mix 1 tsp. of mild liquid hand dishwashing detergent with 1 cup of warm water.
13. **MINERAL OILS.** Your local drug store carries this.
14. **WHITE VINEGAR SOLUTION.** Mix ⅓ cup of white vinegar and ⅔ cup of water.
15. **WHITE VINEGAR – MILD DETERGENT SOLUTION.** Mix a few drops of white vinegar with the MILD DETERGENT SOLUTION (see #13).

NOTE! *Water in solutions should be kept cool to lukewarm.*

TOOLS

1. **COTTON, PAPER, CLOTH & SPONGE.** Have a supply of all of these – absorbent cotton, white facial tissues, white paper towels soft white cloths and sponges. Don't use anything with color in it.
2. **MEDICINE DROPPER.** This ensures you will hit the target with the right amount.

REMOVING STAINS

STAIN TO CLEAN
soft drink, mixed drink, juice, coffee, wine & mud

WEAPONS OF MESS DESTRUCTION
sponge, water, absorbent pads, vinegar - mild detergent solution, alcohol solution, enzyme detergent solution, medicine dropper, chlorine bleach solution, vinegar solution

1. Using a sponge, soak the area with cool to lukewarm water.

2. With an absorbent pad, apply a VINEGAR – MILD DETERGENT SOLUTION.

3. Flush/wash the pad with water to clean it out for the next step.

3. Using the pad, apply the ALCOHOL SOLUTION to the stain. Change the pad as it picks up the stain.

4. Moisten a pad with the ENZYME DETERGENT SOLUTION. Apply it to the stain and leave it for 30 minutes. Keep the stain warm and moistened with the solution.

5. Apply a CHLORINE BLEACH SOLUTION with a medicine dropper. Don't let the solution sit for more than 2 minutes. Flush/wash the area with water after 2 minutes. Apply a VINEGAR SOLUTION to remove the excess chlorine, then flush/wash it again with water.

6. If the stain was on clothes, launder them as soon as possible.

NOTE! Do not use chlorine solution on wool, silk, or spandex.

STAIN TO CLEAN

glues (hobby, contact cement), nail polish, varnish, lacquer, carbon ink

WEAPONS OF MESS DESTRUCTION

sponge, dry-cleaning solvent, several absorbent pads, dry spotter, amyl acetate, medicine dropper, chlorine bleach solution, vinegar solution

1. Sponge the stained area with the DRY-CLEANING SOLVENT. If it's on clothes, put a pad underneath at the same time.

2. Lubricate the pad with DRY SPOTTER (lard or mineral oil also works).

3. Flush/wash the stain with the DRY-CLEANING SOLVENT. Repeat steps 2 and 3 until you see that you are not getting any more stain out.

4. Moisten a pad in AMYL ACETATE and apply it to the stain. Keep the area moist for 15 minutes. Blot it occasionally. Then flush/wash the stained area with the DRY-CLEANING SOLVENT.

5. Using a medicine dropper, apply a CHLORINE BLEACH SOLUTION to remove the final traces of the stain. Don't let the solution sit for more than 2 minutes. Flush/wash the area with water after 2 minutes. Apply a VINEGAR SOLUTION to remove the excess chlorine, then flush/wash it again with water.

NOTE! Do not use chlorine solution on wool, silk, or spandex.

STAIN TO CLEAN

chocolate, ketchup, egg yolk, ice cream, cheese or chilli sauce, gravy, pudding, mayonnaise, meat juice, milk, syrups, vegetable soup

WEAPONS OF MESS DESTRUCTION

Sponge, dry-cleaning solvent, several absorbent pads, dry spotter, medicine dropper, ammonia – mild detergent solution, chlorine bleach solution, vinegar solution, hydrogen peroxide

1. Sponge the stained area with the DRY-CLEANING SOLVENT. If it's on clothes, put an absorbent pad underneath.

2. Lubricate a pad with DRY SPOTTER. Keep the stain moist, changing the pad as it picks up the stain. (You can also lubricate it with a small amount of MINERAL OIL or LARD.)

3. Flush/wash the stained area with the DRY-CLEANING SOLVENT. Let it dry.

4. Use a medicine dropper to apply an AMMONIA – MILD DETERGENT SOLUTION. Flush/wash the stained area with water.

5. Using a medicine dropper, apply a CHLORINE BLEACH SOLUTION to remove any final traces of stain. Don't let the solution sit for more than 2 minutes. Flush/wash the area with water after 2 minutes. Apply a VINEGAR SOLUTION to remove the excess chlorine, then flush/wash it again with water.

6. For chocolate stains, use HYDROGEN PEROXIDE (3%) and add a drop or two of ammonia. Then flush/wash the stained area with water.

NOTE! Do not use chlorine solution on wool, silk, or spandex.

161

LAUNDRY

SORTING

Smaller loads are better. As much as any Dad wants to get laundry done as quickly as possible, it ends up eating a big chunk of one day. Ever since I decided to make the loads smaller and split the laundry chore up over a month, it works a lot easier. Besides, bigger loads wreak havoc on a machine and don't necessarily save costs or time in the long haul.

Manage your family's laundry with more than one laundry basket and one hamper. Use a separate hamper for any clothes that get exposed to pesticides.

1. **GENERAL SORTING.** Separate "lint-givers" (terry towels, cotton sweats, cotton/ramie knits) from "lint-takers" (synthetic blends, smooth, dark or wrinkle-free fabrics). Separate the lightly soiled from the heavily soiled. Separate delicates and wools from non-delicates. Delicates include silk clothes and lingerie. Separate permanent press from everything else. Permanent press clothes include wrinkle free fabrics and those with synthetic fibers excluding acrylic, modacrylic, rayon and acetate. Always keep pesticide-soiled clothing separate from regular laundry. Don't put too many clothes in one wash load. You want your laundry to move freely during the agitation cycle to ensure the best cleaning performance.

2. **UNDERWEAR & SOCKS.** With Kids, this stuff piles up fast.

3. **BATHROOM & KITCHEN TOWELS & FACE CLOTHS.** This is the heavy folding load. Because these items get used everyday, plan to wash them on a semi-regular schedule.

4. **DARKS (& REALLY REDS).** This pile includes anything black, dark blue, dark gray, dark burgundy, dark green or red. Now that detergent manufacturers have come up with a detergent specifically for dark clothes, use them to keep clothes looking darker, longer.

    I feel like a commercial.

5. **WHITES.** These are anything white or have white-background prints that are colorfast. The key here is to avoid including anything with a strong color in it. If something has a very light color in it, but is predominantly white, then you won't have a problem.

6. **COLORS.** Things with patterns and strong colors get thrown into this batch.

NOTE! *Reds like to run. You might want to wash your red stuff with the darks.*

7. **BEDDING.** Sheets, covers and pillow-cases take up a lot of space in the wash. Washing the bedding as a separate load is easier on your machine.

8. **BABY CLOTHES.** These should be washed separately and with a different detergent, which is gentle to both the clothes and the skin of your little one (or more than one).

9. **ICKY.** This would be the category containing rags from your garage and workshop. If you have heavily stained items – coveralls, for example – throw these in this load.

PREPARING CLOTHES

1. Empty the pockets.
2. Check pant legs and sleeves.
3. Close zippers and Velcro® so that fabrics don't snag on each other. Tie loose strings.
4. Turn jeans and dark-colored clothes inside out to prevent color streaking.
5. For Dads with teenage daughters, put their panty hose and items with long ties in a mesh bag so they won't get tangled or torn.
6. Turn T-shirts with screen designs on them inside out so they won't peel.
7. Always check the labels on the clothes for symbols and special instructions. A symbol might tell you that something should be dry-cleaned and not washed.

NOTE! See the SYMBOLS chart on page 166.

PRE-TREATING STAINS

1. Pre-treat stains of washable clothes; take dry-cleanable items to the drycleaner.
2. Pre-soak protein stains in cold water (milk, egg, soybean formula, ice cream, blood and meat juice, or any food stain that contains these ingredients).
3. Use a liquid detergent or pre-treatment spray to take care of oily shirt collars, grease, or oil stains.
4. Don't pre-treat tannin stains with soap (cola drinks, coffee, tea, and fruit juice). Soap will make these stains permanent. ("Tannins" are a plant chemical that produces colors.)
5. Bleach can be used to deal with dye stains from things like felt tip markers. Bleach can also be used on items that are washable, white, or colorfast. Don't soak cottons in bleach solutions for more than 15 minutes.
6. For combination food stains or difficult stains (chewing gum, pencil), check out a stain removal guide. We've covered some of them in this chapter.
7. Use rust remover to treat rust-colored stains. Don't use bleach.
8. Some soap bars are known to take out grass stains. Experiment first on a piece of cloth you don't care about.

DETERGENTS & ADDITIVES

Some people like powders; others like liquids. Dads might prefer the powdered ones that come in packs so that nothing has to be measured. One caveat: products change all the time. I will warn you now to read the directions on any package or bottle. If you have something very special to clean, check with someone you can trust – the people who sell the stuff, a tailor, or even a drycleaner.

1. **LIQUID DETERGENT**. They're good at handling grease and oily stains, and are easier to work with when it comes to pre-treating stains. Usually, they're more expensive, but they work equally well in all water temperatures.

2. **POWDERED DETERGENT**. They cost less to use and seem to work well to lift out clay, mud and ground-in dirt, the kind of dirt accumulated by ground-loving Kids. Powdered detergents have more trouble dissolving in lower water temperatures. So, if you do a lot of cold-water washes, you might want to take this into consideration.

3. **COMBINATION DETERGENT**. They come with multiple personalities: detergent-softener, detergent-bleach. Sometimes, it's easier to use these than having to figure out the use of separate additives, like bleaches and softeners.

4. **LIGHT DUTY DETERGENT**. These are perfect for lightly soiled items and delicate items. If you have a baby, you might want to use this type of detergent. When washing baby's clothes, use detergents without dyes or perfumes to avoid irritating their skin.

5. **DARK DETERGENT**. These were designed to help dark stuff stay darker, longer. If you use the wrong temperature of water (like hot), you will be digging yourself out of a mountain of suds.

6. **LIQUID CHLORINE BLEACH**. It is one of the most effective whiteners and sanitizers. But, it can damage the following: cellulosics (fiber made from plant material, but not synthetic), silk, and wool It can also fade or change the colors of fabrics of any fiber content. Follow the colorfastness test directions on the bleach package to see if it's safe for the fabric you're washing. Never ever pour full-strength, liquid chlorine bleach onto a wash load. It can cause color fading, and weaken fabrics, causing holes or tearing. Don't use liquid chlorine bleach on silk, wool, spandex, polyurethane foam, or rubber.

7. **CONCENTRATED BLEACH SOLUTION**. This solution can weaken cellulosic fibers. Same things happen when you soak cellulosics for too long.

8. **ALL-FABRIC BLEACH**. This is a slower acting bleach that may be safe for colors. Read the package directions carefully. A little bit of this stuff can perk up your darks. If you add the bleach too early during the wash (like I did once), you end up with black jeans sporting a zebra pattern.

9. **FABRIC SOFTENER**. They help reduce clinging, static, and soiling. But, if they're overused, they can reduce the absorbency of towels and diapers, and leave oily looking splotches on medium-colored items.

UNDERSTANDING LOADING & WASHER SETTINGS

1. Start the washing machine before you load anything.

2. Add the detergent. Don't add the bleach until the washer is almost full. Add the softener during the rinse cycle (if you use softener when you wash).

3. Once the detergent has settled into the water, add your clothes.

4. Your clothes should be completely covered with water and no higher than the top of the agitator vanes.

5. Use the highest level for all loads of pesticide-soiled clothes.

6. **CYCLE**. To choose a cycle, you need to understand what kind of load you're working with. The general categories are: regular, permanent press, and delicates. The NORMAL cycle plus HOT or WARM WATER works for soiled and heavier clothing or non-delicate whites. The NORMAL cycle plus COLD WATER is best for dark clothes and clothes in a red color that might have a tendency to run. *NOTE! Consult the CHART on page 166.*

7. **WATER LEVEL**. Most levels are determined by the setting you choose. I thought I'd swim one length further to explain them, so that you could amaze your Kids with this information as you gather laundry together. A 10 to 12 minute wash cycle is needed for regular loads; 8 to 9 minutes for synthetics and knits; 3 to 4 minutes for delicate items and washable wools.

8. **AGITATION**. Heavy-duty agitation helps get out the heavy soils. Slower speeds are used for delicate, lightly soiled items. Too much agitation causes wool to shrink. Too many Kids whining about their laundry causes agitation.

9. **WATER TEMPERATURE**. Hot temps from 120 to 140°F (49 to 60°C) are used for white cottons, underclothes, and pesticide-soiled items. Why? 'Cause hot water kills bacteria. Warm temps from 85 to 105°F (30 to 40°C) are used for synthetics, knits, wrinkle-free or permanent press items. When washing with liquid detergent, cold temps from 65 to 75°F (18 to 24°C) are good for dark or bright-colored clothes and for rinsing. Water temps below 60°F (16°C) are too cold for detergents to work.

DRYING

1. The best rule of thumb to follow is to dry the same load you wash.

2. Don't overload the dryer. Neither the clothes nor the machine wins. Think of it this way. A full load of laundry contains 1 gallon of water going into the dryer. An overloaded dryer also wrinkles clothes something fierce.

3. Clean the lint out of the filter.

4. Add some clean white towels to speed up the drying time of small loads.

5. Turn jeans inside out; they won't fade as much.

6. Don't take the clothes out the moment you hear the buzzer. Let the clothes take advantage of the residual heat during the cool-down period.

LAUNDRY GUIDELINES & SYMBOLS

LOAD	CYCLE	WATER TEMP	DRYER SETTING
whites	regular	hot	normal
colors	regular	warm/cold	normal
permanent press	permanent press	cold	permanent press
delicates	delicates	cold	delicates
wool	delicates	cold	tumble-no heat

Check the labels on your fabrics and clothes for these symbols.

MACHINE WASH INSTRUCTIONS

NORMAL WASH   PERMANENT WASH   GENTLE WASH   DO NOT MACHINE WASH

WATER TEMPERATURE SETTINGS

COLD (<85°F)   WARM (<105°F)   HOT (<120°F)   HOT (<140°F)

SPECIAL CARE

HAND WASH   DO NOT WRING

BLEACHING INSTRUCTIONS

BLEACH AS NEEDED   NON-CHLORINE BLEACH AS NEEDED   DO NOT BLEACH

DRYER INSTRUCTIONS

NORMAL DRY   PERMANENT PRESS   GENTLE WASH   DO NOT TUMBLE DRY

DRYER HEAT SETTINGS

NO HEAT   LOW HEAT   NORMAL MED/HEAT   HIGH HEAT   DO NOT MACHINE DRY

SPECIAL DRYING INSTRUCTIONS

LINE DRY   DRIP DRY   DRY FLAT   DRY IN SHADE

IRONING

LOW HEAT   MODERATE HEAT   HIGH HEAT   DO NOT STEAM   DO NOT IRON

DRY CLEANING

DRY CLEAN   DRY CLEAN WITH ANY SOLVENT   DRY CLEAN WITH PETROLEUM SOLVENT   DRY CLEAN WITH SOLVENTS OTHER THAN TRICHLOROETHYLENE   DO NOT DRY CLEAN.

166

CONCLUSION

DADS FOR LIFE

SURVIVING FOREVER

There is never a last chapter. The most important thing to remember is that –

Dads who love will always be loved!

167

BIOGRAPHIES

CLARENCE SHIELDS

PUBLISHER, ENTREPRENEUR, FATHER OF 3

The original "Culpepper" is one of Alberta's busiest entrepreneurs with interests in publishing, communications and the hotel and gaming industry. After completing university, Clarence joined the family's operations in Fort McMurray, Alberta, to manage several restaurants, including an A & W, which was the first in Canada to generate over 1 million dollars in gross sales. He was a founding member of the "Fort McMurray Academy of Chefs de Cuisine", and spearheaded the first apprenticeship-cooking program at Keyano College in the same city.

Clarence helped develop the first Alberta Food and Beverage Service Training Program and is a former Vice-President of the Alberta Restaurant Association, responsible for Industry Education. Clarence led the project teams that created 2 national best sellers, *The Bachelors Guide™ To Ward Off Starvation* and *The Bachelors Guide™ To Libations*, which have sold over 250,000 copies.

A Father of 3, Clarence remains active with his family and community.

MICHAEL KRYTON

AUTHOR, SCRIPT WRITER

VOICE ARTIST, FATHER OF 4

Michael Kryton has dedicated his life to creativity, working as a professional "creative" for almost 30 years with a diverse skill set that includes writing, directing and producing for radio and television, composing and performing music, as well as performing behind the microphone and in front of the camera. In the latter 80s-early 90s, Michael became a household face in Canada as a notorious television spokesperson for a national consumer electronics chain. He has also produced some of the largest scale, multimedia, live events in Western Canada. His work has garnered awards in Hollywood, New York, Edmonton and Toronto.

This is Michael's first book, having written many scripts and articles over the years as a warm up. Michael has known Clarence for almost 30 years (actually writing his first radio commercials for Clarence's early Alberta operations) and teamed up with him and Yardley to promote the second book in the series, *The Bachelor's Guide™ To Libations*. He continues to be a very active part of the communications industry in Alberta.

Michael is a Father of 4 ranging from 8 to 18, all of whom served as part of the editorial review staff for this book – whether they wanted to or not.

YARDLEY JONES

ILLUSTRATOR, CARTOONIST

PAINTER, FATHER OF 6

Yardley Jones is an internationally renowned illustrator and cartoonist whose work has been requested by Prime Ministers, US Presidents and snubbed by British Royalty. From Canada's Diefenbaker and America's Kennedy, Johnson, Nixon and Clinton, to Britain's Princess Margaret, the Welsh-born artist has been editorializing life and politics since the early 60s, where he began his career after moving from the UK to Canada with his wife in 1957.

Yardley's work has appeared in the Toronto Telegram, the Montreal Star and the Edmonton Journal. Recently, the University of Alberta celebrated his over 45-year career with an exhibition of his work at the University's gallery. Canada Post even immortalized his art on a stamp.

An avid health nut, Yardley, now in his 70s, still runs marathons. Like his marathons, Yardley is never running out of ideas, and continues to paint watercolors, create cartoons, and bring together life and art in his Edmonton studio.

Yardley is a Father of 6 and Grandfather to many.

SPYDER YARDLEY-JONES

ILLUSTRATOR, CARTOONIST

ARTIST IN RESIDENCE, CRAFTSMAN

Spyder Yardley-Jones is continuing to pursue the family's passion and making a name for himself in the process. His art shows in Canada and the US are attracting more attention all the time. When the tattoo-covered artist isn't busy creating caricatures and illustrations for publications and graphic novels, he invests in young minds, conducting workshops and programs, including a literary youth camp called "Youth Write".

His diverse artistic nature is evident on the walls of his home – in every room. Recently, Spyder began to construct eclectic, miniature model 'environments' featuring fantasy-like buildings and working mechanical devices.

Spyder is not yet a Dad, although there are many of his young students who would be very willing to volunteer to be the Kid in his house.

BIBLIOGRAPHY

Food in Early Modern Europe, Ken Alabala [Greenwood Press:Westport CT] 2003

S. Jonathan Bass, *How 'bout a Hand for the Hog': – The Enduring Nature of the Swine as a Cultural Symbol of the South*, Southern Culture, Vol. 1, No. 3, Spring 1995.

Experimental Removal of Stains, M. Wentz, A.C. Lloyd, and A. Watt, Textile Chemist and Colorist, Vol. 7, No. 10, p. 30/179 – 34/183, 1975; Home Methods of Stain Removal, Vivian White, Cornell University, circa 1976 Revised by: Judy L. Price, Cornell Cooperative Extension – Monroe County and Ann T. Lemley, Dept. of Textiles and Apparel, Cornell University, 2002, Judy L. Price, 2005. References: Eastman Kodak Company and Cornell Cooperative Extension – Suffolk County

Consumer Choices: Getting Better Laundry Results, Janis Stone, Iowa State University, University Extension Publication, May 1996

INDEX

172

THE BACHELOR'S GUIDE™ SERIES ORDER FORM

ORDER ONLINE AT WWW.BACHELORSGUIDE.CA

Eggs-citing Ideas, Sandwiches For One, Rabbit Food (Salads), 20+ Ways To Cook Hamburger, Poor Man's Potluck, Career Path Casseroles, Microwave Cooking, Economically Serving Seafood, BBQ Bonanza, Quiet Dinners For 2, Cooking For Six To Eight, Tempting Desserts, Inexpensive Party Treats, Fruit Of The Vine Wines, Getting Started, Cooking Tools and Terms, Spices Of Life, 53 Thrifty Free Suggestions

The Bachelor's Guide™ To Ward Off Starvation, has sold over 250,000 copies. Its 176 pages are filled with recipes, tips, and humor in a language that any bachelor will appreciate. The Guide is the perfect gift for the single man out there looking for the perfect woman.

Beer, Wine & Port, Champagne, The Hard Stuff – Whiskey, Gin, Rum, Vodka, Martinis, Tequila, Cocktails, Shooters, Non-alcoholic, 10 Best Pickup Lines, How You Know You Have A Bite, Lines So Bad They Might Work, Party Ideas, Party Checklist, Glasses, Bachelor's Glasses, Toasts, Hangover Cures

The Bachelor's Guide™ To Libations, another national best seller, is a must read for any bachelor who entertains. This 126-page mix (and twist) on surviving and imbibing is, bar-none, an essential tool for the bachelor who likes to party.

The Father's Guide™ To Surviving with Kids!

Now that you have one, get one for a Dad in need, INDEED!

The Bachelor's Guide™ to Ward Off Starvation at $16.95 C (15.95 USD) # of books ordered _____
The Bachelor's Guide™ to Libations at $9.95 C (8.95 USD) # of books ordered _____
The Father's Guide™ to Surviving with Kids! at $16.95 C (15.95 USD) # of books ordered _____

Add $6.00 C ($5.50 USD) (total order) for shipping and handling. In Canada, add 6% GST.

NAME: _____
STREET/APT: _____
CITY: _____
PROVINCE or STATE: _____
COUNTRY: _____
ZIP CODE or POSTAL CODE: _____

Please make your cheque or money order payable to:
Baytree Holdings Ltd. P.O. Box 1233, Nisku, Alberta, Canada T9E 8A8
Phone 1-780-990-9777   Toll-free US & Canada 1-800-372-7611